Haptic Sensation and Consumer Behaviour

Margot Racat · Sonia Capelli

Haptic Sensation and Consumer Behaviour

The Influence of Tactile Stimulation in Physical and Online Environments

Margot Racat
Mind Your Sense Consulting
Lyon, France

Sonia Capelli
University of Lyon, Iaelyon School of Business, Magellan Research Lab
Lyon, France

ISBN 978-3-030-36924-8   ISBN 978-3-030-36922-4 (eBook)
https://doi.org/10.1007/978-3-030-36922-4

© The Editor(s) (if applicable) and The Author(s), under exclusive license to Springer Nature Switzerland AG 2020
This work is subject to copyright. All rights are solely and exclusively licensed by the Publisher, whether the whole or part of the material is concerned, specifically the rights of translation, reprinting, reuse of illustrations, recitation, broadcasting, reproduction on microfilms or in any other physical way, and transmission or information storage and retrieval, electronic adaptation, computer software, or by similar or dissimilar methodology now known or hereafter developed.
The use of general descriptive names, registered names, trademarks, service marks, etc. in this publication does not imply, even in the absence of a specific statement, that such names are exempt from the relevant protective laws and regulations and therefore free for general use.
The publisher, the authors and the editors are safe to assume that the advice and information in this book are believed to be true and accurate at the date of publication. Neither the publisher nor the authors or the editors give a warranty, expressed or implied, with respect to the material contained herein or for any errors or omissions that may have been made. The publisher remains neutral with regard to jurisdictional claims in published maps and institutional affiliations.

Cover illustration: © John Rawsterne/patternhead.com

This Palgrave Pivot imprint is published by the registered company Springer Nature Switzerland AG
The registered company address is: Gewerbestrasse 11, 6330 Cham, Switzerland

To the goodness of taking time, I dedicate this book to my family who have been the most patient to me and supportive either directly or indirectly when I was on the other side of the world.
—Margot Racat

I dedicate this book to William, Tristan, Hugo and Chiara, who, although in my real physical environment, have seen me leave far too often in the virtual environment of this book.
—Sonia Capelli

Acknowledgements

We would like to thank the editors of Palgrave Macmillan for their interest in our work, patience and kindness during the writing of this book, in particular Liz Barlow.

We also thank the various laboratories that have hosted our research over the past five years on the role of touch in virtual environments: the Magellan Research Center at the iaelyon, and in particular the members of the marketing team, the laboratory at HEC Montréal, especially with Danilo Dantas, and the Consumer Sensory Lab with Maureen Morrin and her team.

Introduction

> "*How do we interact with things in the real world? Well, we pick them up, we touch them with our fingers, we manipulate them. We should be able to do the same thing with virtual objects. We should be able to reach out and touch them*", says Jamie Shotton from Microsoft Research.

Looking at our daily actions and interactions for almost two decades, physical and virtual environments have been merging little by little rather than remaining separated (Milgram et al. 1994), implying a different sensory perception of products as suggested by Jamie Shotton. Accordingly, consumers' direct perception of products in « virtual » environments has become a managerial issue of importance due to the limited stimulation of consumers' senses in online environments. Along with the development of Internet, Internet of Things, Artificial Intelligence and today Robotic, companies and marketers have been constantly challenged for reinventing their way to deliver close and particular experiences to their customers by taking advantages of technology development. In this sense, academic research early explored channelling issues to understand and anticipate how consumer behaviour would be modified in these *a priori* dual environments. First business and marketing approaches had strong opposed views on the possible impact of Internet on business models and how consumer behaviour would evolve. Yet, this first stream of research implicitly took into consideration technical issues while technology itself developed faster than expected or imagined by the market. Thus, in a short period of time, between 2000 and 2005, electronic market started to be a new place to sell products inducing new apprehensions of proximity between products and customers, which became mediated by an interface (i.e. computer at first, tablet and smartphone later on).

A computer-mediated system, being an interface, calls for interaction with an intermediary that is not directly related to the products in terms of intrinsic characteristics. An interface is, similarly to the physical store, a structure that allows one to access to the product, which is in this case virtualized and not tangible anymore. Thus, considering the senses, marketers have been facing a deeper problem than just selling through these interfaces but rather how they would be able to transmit the correct information through, using the consumers' cognitive and perceptual systems. These problematics have been even more of importance since the past ten years and the technological evolution, or revolution as it is now considered. Indeed, interfaces have become more than just a "door" to the virtual environment to be merged with our physical reality. In this configuration, the customer interacts constantly without being really aware of it, i.e. behaving between physical and virtual realities and objects. In particular, and compared to the view and audition, the sense of touch has been widely postponed in these environments from the marketing perspective as being an "aside" sense that could not be stimulated. However, other forms of touch-based stimulation based on (re)emerging theories have been able to reassemble this fragmented apprehension of whole product information processing in those virtual and mediated environments.

Accordingly, this book offers an overview of haptic perception in these dual and soon to merge consumption environments. In Chapter 1, we provide an overview of "what is touching" and explain its characteristics—i.e. "how do we touch". In line with it, we show the explicit and implicit influence the sense of touch has on our perceptual system and mind—i.e. information processing, and particularly how these influences modify consumers' behaviour. We then expose in Chapter 2 the new consumer journeys through digital interfaces and review part of the literature on virtual environments and afferent notions that are virtual and augmented reality to position the new consumers' experience through interfaces as well as the change in consumption habits. In Chapter 3, we define and explain the different type of tactile interfaces currently available on the market. We further discuss the tactile rendering techniques and benefits from a consumer's perspective for online shopping. Finally, in Chapter 4, we provide a set of research with specific examples that support the development of the previous chapters. It particularly focuses on recent and relevant research on haptics interfaces (development and consumer approach) as well as it will develop a first-hand research study with materials that lie down foundation to consider for future haptic interface in consumption.

Reference

Milgram, Paul, Haruo Takemura, Akira Utsumi, and Fumio Kishino. 1994. "Augmented Reality: A Class of Displays on the Reality-Virtuality Continuum." In *Telemanipulator and Telepresence Technologies*, edited by Hari Das, 2351, 282–92. https://doi.org/10.1117/12.197321.

Contents

1 Introduction to the World of Haptic Sensations   1
  1.1 The Sense of Touch   2
    1.1.1 Social and Cultural Dimensions   3
    1.1.2 Neuro-Psychophysical Dimensions   7
  1.2 Tactile Stimulation, a Consumer and Product Perspective   11
    1.2.1 Consumers' Individual Characteristics for Touching   11
    1.2.2 Product Tactile Cues   15
    1.2.3 Consumer Interpretation of Product Tactile Properties   19
  1.3 Conclusion   22
  References   23

2 Touching Without Touching: The Paradox of the Digital Age   33
  2.1 Internet Environment: Evolution of Consumers' Experience with Products   34

		2.1.1 New Consumers' Experience: Online Image Interactivity	35
		2.1.2 Mediated Environments: Human–Machine Interactions	38
	2.2	Impact of Mediated Environments on Consumers' Product Perception	47
		2.2.1 Multichannel Shopping Environments: Enhancing Sensory Interactions	47
		2.2.2 Visuo-Haptic Stimulation in Online Shopping Environments	50
	2.3	Conclusion	51
	References		52
3	**When Interfaces Make It Real**		**65**
	3.1	From Product Touch to the Interface Touch	66
		3.1.1 Interface Haptic Stimulation and Influence on Consumers' Behaviour	66
		3.1.2 Consumers' Evolution of Touching in Computer-Mediated Environments	69
	3.2	Tactile Rendering Systems: Recovering Haptic Experiences	71
		3.2.1 Tactile Rendering Technologies: Functioning and Developments	72
		3.2.2 Realism for Consumption Environments: Visual and Haptic Rendering of Texture	78
	3.3	Managerial Focus: From Imagination to Sensory Stimulation	82
	3.4	Conclusion	84
	References		84
4	**The Future of Consumption in a Haptic-Based World**		**95**
	4.1	To Mimic or Not to Mimic the Reality? That Is the Question	96
		4.1.1 Congruency and Similarity in Mediated Environments	97

		4.1.2	Online Sensory Information Processing: An Experimental Plan	101
	4.2		Implication for the Future of Haptic Consumption	109
References				112

Conclusion   117

Index   119

List of Figures

Fig. 1.1	Touch in consumption environments	23
Fig. 2.1	Continuum of mixed reality (Adapted from Milgram et al. 1994)	40
Fig. 3.1	List of current main haptic rendering systems	73
Fig. 3.2	Tactile classification of devices based on consumers' haptic interaction (*Source* [a]Image parOpenClipart-Vectors de Pixabay—Free of use. [b]Image parhamonazaryan1 de Pixabay—Free of use. [c]Image parNiek Verlaan de Pixabay—Free of use. [d]Image parPexels de Pixabay—Free of use. [e]Image by Free-Photos de Pixabay—Free of use)	74
Fig. 4.1	Research model adapted from Racat and Capelli (2016)	102
Fig. 4.2	Results of study 1	104
Fig. 4.3	Stimulus in 3D	106
Fig. 4.4	Interface tactile stimuli—study 1	107

List of Tables

Table 1.1	Items of the comfort with interpersonal touch scale (Webb and Peck 2015)	5
Table 1.2	Role of skin receptors	10
Table 1.3	Product classification based on sensory approach	16
Table 2.1	Interface haptic stimulation	44
Table 2.2	Presence and telepresence definitions	45
Table 3.1	Classification of tactile interfaces based on haptic rendering system	75
Table 3.2	Overview of Lederman, Klatzky and their colleagues research exploring haptic perception through non-tactile rendering devices	76

1

Introduction to the World of Haptic Sensations

Abstract This chapter aims to position the sense of touch within the consumption context. The authors first define the sense of touch from cultural, sociological, psychological, and marketing perspectives. The authors provide an overview of the academic research of "what is touching" and explain its characteristics—i.e. "how do we touch". Then the authors show the explicit and implicit influence the sense of touch has on our perceptual system and mind—i.e. information processing. At the end of the chapter, the authors expose how it influences consumers' direct experience of product in store environments.

Keywords Touching · Consumption · Physiology · Need for touch · Diagnostic

This chapter aims to position the sense of touch within the consumption context. The authors first define the sense of touch from cultural, sociological, psychological, and marketing perspectives. The authors provide an overview of the academic research of "what is touching" and explain its characteristics—i.e. "how do we touch". Then the authors show the explicit and implicit influence the sense of touch has on our perceptual system and mind—i.e. information processing. At the end of the chapter, the authors expose how it influences consumers' direct experience of product in store environments.

1.1 The Sense of Touch

Touch is a fascinating sense since, without it, human beings would hardly live in the environment. Without the sense of touch, one would have greater difficulties to understand the world, connect to others, and simply move along this same environment. As a matter of fact, the sense of touch is also the first to develop during the process of becoming a small and fresh cute, or not, newborn. As such, Montagu (1971) deeply demonstrates how it enables any human to perceive the world from the very beginning of life to its end. While being in the mother's wombs, a newborn can feel and perceive tactile sensations related to what is surrounding him. Touch is also the life longest sense to be efficient when the visual, auditory, olfactory and gustatory system tends to decrease drastically and rapidly after a certain age.

The sense of touch is defined by several components that consist of structural and psychophysical characteristics but also by one's culture and social environment that deeply influence, in the long term, tactile apprehension and its development. For instance, medical research early showed that nursing newborn by holding them regularly enables the tactile system to better develop with finer dimensions than rarely being in contact (Reite 1990). In line with it, Harry Harlow's[1] controversial research demonstrated the importance of tactile dimension in babies' development: a small baby monkey rather preferred being surrounded by a wired mother having warm tactile clothes than a wired mother without these tactile cues but enabling feeding. In his attempt to understand the nature

---

[1] See for the complete article: http://psychclassics.yorku.ca/Harlow/love.htm.

of love, his experiments showed that tactile need is deeper and stronger than apparently vital elements.

On a psychological side, touch can provide long-term benefits such as healing or reducing stress compared to barely tactile behaviour that turns out to increase depressive and negative overall thinking behaviour (Field 1998). As a matter of fact, what needs to be kept in mind is the broad influence that touch has on the definition of our existence, and by such, how deep it defines our attitude, emotions and behaviour.

1.1.1 Social and Cultural Dimensions

Literal definition of the action of "touching" refers to "putting one's hand in contact with something or somebody to appreciate its state, consistency, warmth, etc." (Le Petit Larousse Illustré 2010, p. 1020; Encyclopédie Bordas) while the name "Touch" refers to the sense that enables physical perception of objects, pressure, cold and warmth, through skin contact. These definitions consider several orders: physical (enter in contact), relational (reach out, communicate), and introspective (affect, feeling). Touching the environment and our surroundings enables to have a conscious understanding that we are not alone but also that we are part of a greater ensemble (Ackerman 1990; Montagu 1971). As such, touch, among the other senses, acts as a mediator of our perception of the environment, and more specifically, touch is the sense dedicated to exploration and openness to the world. Indeed, the sense of touch is a door to the world that demonstrates the tangibility of what is captured by the visual, auditory, olfactory and gustatory systems (Klatzky et al. 1985).

Historically, the sense of touch has been considered and treated as the most primitive sense (Gregory 1967). Yet being the most developed sense from our birth to death (Hertenstein et al. 2006), it is also our finest sense with multiple faces that are hard to verbalise into simple words (Krishna 2010). As such, touch helps to understand and create concreteness but also to conceptualise with finer details (Serino and Haggard 2010). Besides, research from various fields has come to a consensus to situate the first exploration of the sense in the Aristotle era (Jütte 2008, p. 3). However, origins of the integration of touch as a main sense, being at the centre of everything, are located in India and China where religious and medicinal knowledges were based on tactile sensation and perception (for a historical review, see Grundwald 2008; Parisi 2018). Yet Western countries remained for a long time attached to a dissociation of the senses and particularly setting apart tactile interactions for the overall behavioural comprehension (Parisi 2018).

Socially, touching is the sense of contact that brings interactions and connect people and is referred to as interpersonal touch also labelled Midas touch (Willis and Hamm 1980; Gallace and Spence 2010; Webb and Peck 2015; Guest et al. 2009). Extent academic research shows that touch is deeply involved into sexual desire (Nguyen et al. 1975), intimacy (Heslin et al. 1983), compliance (Willis and Hamm 1980; Patterson et al. 1986; Hornik 1992), trust and self-confidence (Peck and Childers 2003a, b), consumption behaviour (Guéguen and Jacob 2005; Martin 2012) and in medical care settings (Whitcher and Fisher 1979). As well, previous studies from the 1980s to 1990s show that touch is related to gender (Willis and Briggs 1992). The authors show that women and men differ in their evaluation of touch according to the provenance and the zone reached out by the touch. For instance, considering personal and intimate relationship between two persons, men have higher potential for initiating tactile interactions for seducing while women have a higher use of touch when the relationship is more formalised. Yet these findings date from the 1980s to 1990s and might need some refreshment; however, what matters in this case is that men are culturally more engaged into tactile interaction for flirting and reaching out to the opposite sex. Similarly, touch can be a social distant barrier and divide people between those who initiate and those who receive the touch (Heslin et al. 1983; Andersen and Leibowitz 1978). When one initiates a tactile behaviour, women first acknowledge the relational aspect with the person (i.e. friends, family, intimacy) while men first considered the gender. Nevertheless, for both women and men, being touched by a person who is a relative and from the opposite sex is considered as pleasant. Another example is the consideration of the implementation of touch: whether it is the hand, the arm of an intimate zone that is reached out, the signification differs between the two individuals that are interacting (Nguyen et al. 1975). Indeed, touch can be either perceived as intrusive if it comes from a total stranger (Heslin et al. 1983) or welcomed in the case of stressful situation where a relative initiates the touch that, as a consequence, tends to reduce anxiety and calm down the person (Grewen et al. 2003). Accordingly, interpersonal touch can be a form of pleasure, adventure and arousal depending on the region, gender and intentionality. However, reading these findings, one needs to keep in mind that it must be replaced in the context of studies that dates for most of them from the 1970s to 1990s. With cultural and moral changes that occurred during the past twenty years, it needs to be further investigated.

Nevertheless, the tactile system in itself shows that touch is a matter of distance and intimacy between two persons and is positively considered when the persons are not total strangers, even though men would be less reluctant anyhow. As well, it is important to consider the cultural aspect of these interpretations; for a long time now, we know that differences exist in tactile behaviours between countries: in southern cultures, it is common to generate rather tactile behaviours (e.g. Latin), as shaking hands and kissing, while the more it goes to northern countries the more distance is required between people (e.g. North American) (Mooij et al. 2011; Mooij and Hofstede 2010; Hofstede 1983; Remland et al. 1995). These differences of approaches to the tactile connection have been captured by Webb and Peck (2015) with the definition of the *comfort with interpersonal touch* scale that allows to differentiate between initiating and receiving touch. Their research allows to position most people regarding their individual preference for touching people or being touched (Table 1.1)

Table 1.1 Items of the comfort with interpersonal touch scale (Webb and Peck 2015)

Initiating touch dimension	Receiving touch dimension
• I consider myself to be a more "touchy" person than most of my friends	• I don't mind if someone touches my arm
• I feel more comfortable initiating touch than most people	• During conversation, I don't mind if people touch me
• When talking to people, I often touch them on the arm	• I typically don't mind receiving touch from another person

Last but not least, religious considerations position touch as a sin, which is true in all three monotheist religions inducing prohibition and is part of the reason why the sense of touch received less attention in our modern society than the others senses. We won't dig into this aspect of touch and for a further understanding of the religious impact one can refer to specialised literature. Yet it is worth mentioning since it influences behaviours and by doing so, consumption. Indeed, the religious moral and prohibition lead to order the senses in a way that the more a sense seems to be distant the purest it is. As such, the sense of touch and taste has been considered as inferior since easy to access by anyone. On the contrary, distant senses as the vision, auditory and olfactory have been glorified and set up as pure (Parisi 2018). As such, touch is, by essence, related to the material and earth. The tangibility of labour through the work of the soil has been associated with impureness and dirtiness (Coulmas 2012). Yet with all this historical background, an article from the *Stuttgarter Nachrichten, edited on October 18th, 1999*, declared that we entered the age of haptic perceptions (Grundwald 2008) that today's technology definitely emphasises.

In 2019, we clearly observe the necessity to consider the tactile interactions in every actions and environments. In only two decades, the development and use of interfaces have created a new space where people have been disconnected from their perception but socially more connected than ever (Cummins et al. 2014). Paradoxically, most of the semantic language used in these environments to connect people refers to tactile and physical interactions (e.g. getting in touch). Yet the majority of people seeks for proximity, human contact and contact with the nature (Cascio et al. 2019). One example in the Western world is the development of "natural" medicine such as chiropractors and magnetism in almost a decade only. With the mediation of communication technologies, touching becomes even more important in every aspect of one's life: social, health and consumption (Citrin et al. 2003). From this observation, numerous business have opened in less than ten years to connect people to the reality and to keep contact with tangible representation of their online social life (Smith 2009). Since approximately 2013, cats bar or cuddle café has raised in Europe and represents a tendency that demonstrates the growing need for tactile interactions. Funny enough, this observation had been underlined in the 1940s by Revesz (Grundwald 2008, p.12) who stated that touching was important in the processing of information and that this way was the only one to be trustful and convincing.

Consequently, the evolution of mentalities and progress in technology emphasises today how much the proximity and direct contact represent the challenge but, more than ever, the crucial need of the current century and the next to come: touch is at the centre of every relationship whether it is between people and objects, in physical and mediated environments.

1.1.2 Neuro-Psychophysical Dimensions

Contrary to the definition provided above that suppose that touching is an action of the hand only, from a structural viewpoint, it must be considered that the entire human body is a tactile receptor that enables to perceive spatial orientation, balance, speed and feel internal and external tactile sensations (Montagu 1971; Grundwald 2008; Parisi 2018; Ackerman 1990). Sensations are what tactile receptors receive while we are interacting with our environment, somebody or something. Specifically, a sensation is the physical stimulation of one or several receptors which becomes an information. Once a receptor is stimulated, it involves a treatment of it that goes through the perceptual system. Thus, perception processes information such as it discriminates, interprets and transmits the received information to the brain for a second-order treatment that will trigger other physiological reactions, mental and behavioural answers (Zwaan 1999; Barsalou 2008, 2010). Overall, the reception and transmission of this information are supported by a central nervous system that connects the entire body to the brain (Borghi and Pecher 2012). For this reason, any part of our body as well as any organs is a sensory receptor that brings information and enables us to react (for a detailed review, see Grundwald 2008). Regarding the sense of touch, academic research has come along to identify somatosensory areas in the brain and determined the most sensitive parts of our body. For instance, the homunculus first modelled by Penfield and Boldrey (1937) represents a broad illustration of the repartition of our perceptual system that is based on tactile sensations. Yet this representation still needs finer completion since scientific knowledge has evolved on this matter.

From this representation, we can observe the importance of hands and mouth. Even though skin is more important in terms of size, hands and mouth constitute the organs that enable us to receive and reach the outside to internalise it. Studies on these organs, and more specifically hands, have come to dissociate into two main dimensions of our tactile perception: the passive and active ways, the latest being also known as haptic system (Klatzky et al. 1991; Yazdanparast and Spears 2012). Passive tactile perception relies on tactile stimulation that is, for most of the time, unconsciously received. Skin is an emblematic receptor that enables exteroceptive sensations—i.e. to sense any external elements that come into contact with the body (Fuchs and Moreau 2003, p. 162). Therefore, passive tactile perception mostly relies on external and non-intentional tactile stimulation and is constantly stimulated, but does not draw continuous active attention. Active touch or haptic perception designates the procurement of information via intentional use of touch. The origin of "haptic" word comes from the Greek that is "haptikos" and means "ability to put one's hand on"; in other words, it suggests that touch is intrinsically related to action (Révész 1950; Gibson 1962). However, "haptic" is also recognised to have been introduced by Max Dessoir (1867–1947) who suggested a rather global word—*haptisch*—to entail all forms of tactile sensations and mechanisms that can be associated with the sense of touch. As a newer form for naming touch, it enables to consider broader and finer distinctions of what is "touch" such as haptic enables to "capture, order, map, and represent the variety of sensations formerly grouped messily together under the heading of touch" (Parisi 2018, p. 143). Especially, Dessoir's denomination further enables to differentiate from the external (hands, mouth, skin, etc.) that would be tactility and the internal receptors (joints, muscles) that would be haptic (Grundwald 2008; Parisi 2018). In line with it, the haptic system is a combination of two main receptors: cutaneous and kinaesthetic (or proprioceptive) that comprise limbs, joints and muscles (Lederman and Klatzky 1987). For instance, when an individual grasps a product to smell it, it uses both passive and active touch. Here, the sense of touch is activated through the haptic system that includes the passive form: besides smelling, the person can feel the texture, weight the product, detect its contours, as well as its temperature, without being the first conscious objective. In this case, touch is not actively solicited but passively used by transmitting information. Therefore, passive and active forms of touch play a considerable role in our understanding of the external world by constantly keeping us aware of our surroundings, whether it is conscious or not. Moreover, compared to the other senses, it is both a pro and reactive sense. As well, maybe for this reason, numerous academic but also non-academic writings use interchangeably the terms haptic and tactile to designate the sense of touch and its mechanisms and process (Parisi 2018).

This unique characteristic of touch emphasises the importance for being considered into marketing practices as well as the fact that, unlike to others senses, touch brings information along without interruption— i.e. it is not possible to shut down the sense of touch as it is for the others: closing the eyes (visual), holding the nose (olfactory and gustatory) and covering the ears (auditory). Therefore, touch brings information day and night and constantly influences our perception of the environment and how we connect with it. But then, how does touch bring information along? The constant connection to the environment leads to question the role of touch and how it works fundamentally since in a consumption environment it will *a priori* impact our perception as well.

Grasping an object to analyse and evaluate is a common behaviour that occurs without conscious thinking. Indeed, as introduced above, hands are the most obvious organs representing the sense of touch that we deal with and use in our daily interactions. The hands have a complex internal linkage of mechanical, thermal and nociceptors (joints, muscles and nerves ending) that provide a very fine level of information at which the sense of touch operates to explore objects and provide understanding (Lederman and Klatzky 1987). More precisely, researchers differentiate tactile receptors based on their level of tactile sensitivity. In particular, the sensitivity is related to the location within the skin and the subcutaneous tissues. Receptors are defined as either free nerves endings (i.e. cutaneous and kinaesthetic) or joints, muscles and nerves (i.e. kinaesthetic) that are connected to the central nervous system. Accordingly, researchers have come to distinguish mechanoreceptors, thermoreceptors and nociceptors as being specialised receptors for, respectively, contact forces, temperature and painful stimulation

Besides, each receptor has two characteristics based on (1) the capacity of the fibres to adapt fast or slowly (commonly labelled FA or SA) and (2) the reception field capacity (type I—small or type II—large) (Lederman and Klatzky 2009). Adaptation describes how much static or dynamic is the receptor to react for sending information according to tactile changes while the field of reception allows the detection of sharp or wider distortion of the skin (Table 1.2).

Based on this, we observe that haptic perception activates the overall type of receptors. As we daily use our limbs to move and interacts, haptic becomes important when considering consumption and shopping environment since in these environments, consumers are active to choose and purchase products. More specifically, haptic perception allows consumers to obtain tactile information that are translated to the brain, and this tactile behaviour is directed by the individual preferences and by the environment that both lead to haptic exploration of products.

Table 1.2 Role of skin receptors

Receptor	Location	Main sensitivity	Type	Speed and adaptation
Meissner corpuscles	Dermis	Contact, pressure	Cutaneous	Fast (FA I)
Merkel disks	Epidermis	Stretching, pressure	Cutaneous	Slow (SA I)
Ruffini organ	Dermis	Stretching, pressure	Mechanical	Slow (SA II)
Krause bulbs	Dermis	Vibrations, pressure	Mechanical	Fast (FA II)
Pacinian corpuscle	Hypodermis	Vibrations, pressure	Mechanical	Fast (FA II)
Golgi joints	Joints, muscles	Tension, movement	Mechanical	–

1.2 Tactile Stimulation, a Consumer and Product Perspective

While shopping in store, buyers are generally more attracted by products that are accessible and with which it is possible to interact, in particular for product with high tactile cues (Klatzky and Peck 2012; McCabe and Nowlis 2003). Accordingly, in-store product presentations have evolved towards product exhibition enabling consumers to touch and test them before purchasing (e.g. Nature & Découvertes, Sephora, etc.). Handling products enables a greater sensory experience that is overall enabled by haptic apprehension: by taking in hand a product, a consumer can smell, look closer, listen to and even taste the product. As well, handling the product in store enables to further explore it with hands.

Therefore, the environment and the product are elements that influence consumers' behaviour by bringing furthermore tactile information, either consciously or not (Peck and Childers 2006). As a consequence, brands deeply rolled into the understanding and use of consumers' sensory experience once they understood the deep impact it has on overall evaluation and purchase behaviours (Krishna 2010; Lindstrom 2005). Accordingly, in this second section, we give interest to the tactile influence on consumption behaviour based on consumers' individual characteristics and products tactile cues.

1.2.1 Consumers' Individual Characteristics for Touching

Peck and Childers (2003a) as well as Citrin et al. (2003) came along the same year with two approaches of the need for touch (NFT) and need for tactile input (NTI) in shopping environments. These two approaches enable brands and managers to understand the potential tactile behaviour of their customers and thus enable them to anticipate an appropriate environment or solutions for accessing their products. In particular, the NFT scale has been of major use in the marketing literature although other scales early considered the dual approach for touching product in physical and virtual environments as for the NTI.

1.2.1.1 Need for Touch

Peck and Childers (2003a) define the NFT as an individual preference for haptic information. More precisely, it is the *preference for the extraction and utilisation of information obtained through the haptic system* (p. 431). The NFT is grounded in motivations rather than abilities and thus based on cultural and social norms. Moreover, based on hedonic and utilitarian research for consumption (Holbrook and Hirschman 1982; Hirschman and Holbrook 1982), the authors defined and developed a two-dimensional scale that relies on the instrumental (i.e. informational) and autotelic (i.e. hedonic) dichotomy. Instrumental NFT dimension refers to a purchasing goal-driven touch for seeking information while shopping to obtain evaluative outcomes. Autotelic NFT refers to the fun, fantasy and sensory arousal hedonic profile of consumption such as touching is an end in itself. We present below the scale items according to the two dimensions (Peck and Childers 2003a):

Autotelic Need For Touch

- When walking through stores, I can't help touching all kinds of products,
- Touching products can be fun,
- When browsing in stores, it is important for me to handle all kinds of products,
- I like to touch products even if I have no intention of buying them,
- When browsing in stores, I like to touch lots of products,
- I find myself touching all kinds of products in stores.

Instrumental Need For Touch

- I place more trust in products that can be touched before purchase,
- I feel more comfortable purchasing a product after physically examining it,
- If I can't touch a product in the store, I am reluctant to purchase the products,
- I feel more confident making a purchase after touching a product,

- The only way to make sure a product us worth buying is to actually touch it,
- There are many products that I would only buy if I could handle them before purchase.

1.2.1.2 Need for Tactile Input

Citrin et al. (2003) define the NTI as a tactile stimulation that is necessary for the consumer while shopping over the Internet. The authors state that the higher the NTI for making product/brand choices the less likely an individual is to make online purchase due to the absence of tactile interactions. The NTI relies on informational objectives related to Internet usage and gender issues on tactile behaviour, which goes in line with cultural and social aspect of touch, as well as the type of product concerned. We present below the scale items defined by Citrin et al. (2003):

Need for Tactile Input

- I need to touch a product in order to evaluate its quality.
- I need to touch a product in order to evaluate how much I will like the product.
- I feel it necessary to touch a product in order to evaluate its physical characteristics.
- I feel it is necessary to touch a product in order to evaluate its quality.
- I need to touch a product in order to evaluate its physical characteristics.
- I need to touch a product in order to create a general evaluation of it.

1.2.1.3 Interface Need for Touch

Considering both scales almost two decades after, we can see that the NFT scale was created to determine tactile behaviours for in-store shopping experience and does not entirely fit with the virtual environments that are now considered. Indeed, the current consideration of touch relates to the interface tactile cues as an entire part of haptic processing, whether the interface is tactile or not (i.e. mouse vs. touchscreen). As well, the NTI scale, although considering more the Internet as a shopping environment, failed to integrate the interface as potential medium for tactile input while Alba et al. (1997) demonstrated the importance of considering the potential technological development that would fast change the Internet shopping behaviour. Yet both scale propositions remain of importance regarding individual characteristics and even more of interest considering today's stimulation of the tactile sense in virtual environments through the interfaces (Jin 2011; Brasel and Gips 2014). Moreover, the Internet and its afferent interfaces lead to merge the environments and modify tactile interactions between the consumer and the product, which in turn influences differently consumers' decision-making process by integrating different channel to access the product (Chapter 2) when the interfaces are not yet ready to render tactile sensations (Chapter 3). Consequently, both scales help for understanding consumers' preferences for using tactile dimension in consumption and shopping behaviours. However, Peck and Childers (2003a) have been more precise on the motivational aspect helping managers to define the way to present product to their consumers while the scale from Citrin et al. (2003) helps for understanding a more general tendency from a consumer for touching a product based on personal feeling and arousal. Yet both are in need for further investigation to adapt to the dual environments (i.e. physical-virtual environments), but also new haptic environments, that both studies underlined as being a future challenge to come and that today it is a clear matter of importance in consumption.

Indeed, so far, no other scale of that sort and of our knowledge has been developed and it seems that the question of the virtual tactile sensations is still a hot topic question to be determined. The question raised here is then based on Peck and Childers (2003a) definition of NFT and Citrin et al. (2003) NTI, which emphasises that any individual has tactile preference and that the environment plays a major role to allow consumers to access and use tactile inputs. As such, for the past ten years, research came along with new considerations of the interface and its tactile cues and of course its influence on consumers' tactile perception of the online experience of the environment, product and social interactions (Brasel and Gips 2015) (Chapter 2). Yet before reaching the next chapter, we counterbalance the tactile characteristic of the consumer with those of the products that play a major role in eliciting tactile behaviours in consumption environments.

1.2.2 Product Tactile Cues

1.2.2.1 Product Classification

In marketing, it exists different possibilities to classify and categorise products along tactile cues. Mostly, these classifications rely on the functionalities and type of products (e.g. what utilisation and how it works) (McCabe and Nowlis 2003) or based upon sensory properties (Klatzky and Lederman 1993). Both categorisations rely on intrinsic and extrinsic definition of the product that marketers must determine when developing a new offer. Intrinsic cues refer to the product physical attributes (i.e. design, shape, texture, weight, etc.) while the extrinsic cues refer to the conceptual and extended level of the product definition (i.e. brand, product name, price, etc.) (Achrol and Kotler 2012). Within the product intrinsic cues definition, the marketing literature distinguishes two more specific categories based on the geometric and material properties for which the marketing literature seems to have a consensus as shown in Table 1.3.

Another way to classify products is based on their functions and on the type of information that is searched at first stand (McCabe and Nowlis 2003). However, in the end, products are defined by their sensory properties that provoke individual elicitation to touch the product whether it is offline or online (Klatzky and Peck 2012). Therefore, the product tactile cues are of major interest since without its material representation in the physical environment, it would not exist from a haptic perspective.

Table 1.3 Product classification based on sensory approach

Categorisation	Authors	Conclusions
Geometric or **material**	Klatzky et al. (1993)	The geometric characteristic is related to the shape or size of the product and involves more sight while the material attribute is related to touch to more precisely determine the texture of the product, its hardness-solidity, roughness, weight, temperature or the components of the product (detachable or not)
Digital or **non-digital**	Lal and Sarvary (1999)	The so-called digital elements of the product can be digitised and transposed into a virtual, dematerialised environment, without obstructing a meaning (written information, photo). The so-called non-digital attributes of the product imply that they are difficult to transpose and hide part of the product test unlike a real situation (texture, temperature)
Sensorial or non-sensorial	Degeratu et al. (2000)	Sensory products can be understood only through the senses, while non-sensory products can be described verbally
Hedonic or utilitarian	Dhar and Wertenbroch (2000)	Hedonic products are those whose consumption is mainly based on the affect and senses involved, while utilitarian products are mainly cognitive in terms of research (satisfying a need) and whose objective of information research is more oriented

1.2.2.2 Product Evaluation: Exploratory Procedures

Klatzky et al. (1993) clearly identify the geometric and material properties as two main dimensions that initiate either more visual or haptic exploration for diagnostic purposes. The authors show that product geometric and material properties are appreciated differently by the sensory system: while geometric properties are predominantly considered by the visual system, the material properties are predominantly considered by the haptic system (Lederman and Klatzky 1987). The same researchers came to label the haptic system as being an "expert system" (Klatzky et al. 1985) that uses "exploratory procedures" (Lederman and Klatzky 1987). Exploratory procedures are hand movements with the explicit intention to search for specific information about the product. Besides, the more an object is common and integrated in our daily life, the faster it is for consumers to recognise it without seeing it, which demonstrates the fine expertise system.

However, in normal condition of explorations, the visual sense is as much dominant, yet to be blind or diminished. Thus, both senses are interrelated and complementary (Serino and Haggard 2010) and sometimes act as biased to each other (Krishna 2006). Nevertheless, the haptic system uses a specialised encoding pathway that brings finer conceptualisation and mental representations (Serino and Haggard 2010), for product substance (i.e. material: hardness, roughness, smoothness, temperature) (Klatzky et al. 1985). Therefore, considering the product perspective, three ways of apprehension exists: visual exploration, semi-visual and haptic exploration (Klatzky et al. 1993; Klatzky and Lederman 1993). Haptic system uses either one way or the three ways for exploration, depending on the availability of the visual sense, but mostly, the haptic system is necessary upon the product tactile cues salience (Heller 1982). Yet even though visual apprehension comes first and tends to enhance the touch effect, haptic exploration is finer and provides more reliable evaluation, precision for diagnostic purposes (Klatzky et al. 1987; Serino and Haggard 2010).

1.2.2.3 Diagnostic Touch and Non-diagnostic

Regarding the product tactile cues, one consideration that research on haptic exploration has evidenced is the diagnostic role of touch (Yazdanparast and Spears 2012, 2013). As described above, if a product is based on material properties, the use of touch becomes necessary to fully understand its characteristics and its use. In this case, the haptic exploration becomes a diagnostic touch while when the touch is mostly a complement, it is a non-diagnostic touch that still has an influence on consumer's evaluation and behaviour (Peck and Wiggins 2006; Marlow and Jansson-Boyd 2011). For instance, shopping for clothes activates the sense of touch since only tactile information allows to understand and attest of the potential pleasure to wear it (Rahman 2012). Even though literal information is given, confirmation will be necessary through haptic exploration since it contains essential information that is not accessible through the other senses (e.g. softness, confidence into judgement). Nevertheless, non-diagnostic touch is also of importance since it also influences consumers' evaluation as Krishna and Morrin (2008) illustrate it: when consumers test the same mixed water-based drink in a flimsy or firm plastic glass, judgement differs while touch is not a primarily solicited sense for product evaluation. In this case, the tactile information received by the glass material is not essential to understand the content but still influences its evaluation. Thus, handling a product provides tactile sensations that transmit impactful information, even if the product is based on geometrical properties (i.e. computer). Consequently, the diagnostic dimension of touch helps for understanding the product functioning, determines what it is, classifies and evaluates it. In other words, diagnostic touch, that employs exploratory procedures, is related to the product intrinsic characteristics. On the contrary, the non-diagnostic touch doesn't allow this classification neither to categorise the product but rather provides external and unrelated tactile sensations—i.e. tactile stimulation coming from external sources—that are still processed, interpreted and influential, on a positive or negative side, for product evaluation and behavioural answers (Grohmann et al. 2007).

1.2.3 Consumer Interpretation of Product Tactile Properties

1.2.3.1 Adding Tactile Cues to the Product

Previous research dealing with the product tactile properties focuses on texture as tactile lever. Considering previous research on product definition and classification, texture is a major attribute of products definition (Yoshida 1968; Klatzky et al. 1993; Picard et al. 2003; Ekman et al. 1965). Accordingly, Okamoto et al. (2013) define the tactile perception that is inherent to texture apprehension as the "perception of the qualities and properties of material surfaces by touch". However, these psychophysical dimensions of texture are difficult to verbalise with representative words that can enable us to compare on a similar basis our experiences (Okamoto et al. 2013; Krishna 2012). For instance, Yoshida (1968), through semantic differential technique, highlighted that haptic descriptor differences exist between fibre and metal type materials. Yet Okamoto et al. (2013) review of papers on the psychophysical dimensions of tactile perception of texture shows that mostly we perceived and express roughness/smoothness (at macro- and micro-levels), warmness/coldness, hardness/softness and friction (moistness/dryness, stickiness/slipperiness) as major tactual impression when touching a product. Moreover, Soufflet et al. (2004) explored the industrial environment of texture determination and found the same tactual impression dimensions than for consumer research: roughness, thermal and solidity (Giboreau et al. 2001; Okamoto et al. 2013; Skedung et al. 2011). Consequently, most of marketing studies on texturing has been based on these findings to elaborate further understanding of consumer behaviour.

From a consumer research, perspective, texture and more globally product tactile stimulation has either a positive or a negative influence on product evaluation, purchase intention and donation behaviour (Krishna and Schwarz 2014). One major practical example in the marketing universe has been *Coca Cola* emblematic glass bottle (Lindstrom 2005): the company succeeded to establish a deep relation between the tactile attributes (i.e. texture is related to coca leaves groove) and its brand name. On this matter, the brand is a strong sensory brand that uses sensory attributes as tactile and visual cues to enhance consumers' attitude towards the brand. Therefore, the effect of texture is of great importance since it influences product choice and willingness to pay as well as it enhances brand recognition (Streicher and Estes 2015, 2016; Grohmann et al. 2007). Moreover, it also comes to increase consumers' confidence on product evaluation (d'Astous and Kamau 2010), to create greater ownership feelings (Peck and Shu 2009; Shu and Peck 2011) and to generate higher consumers' preference for product that have more material properties (McCabe and Nowlis 2003). Finally, texture also comes to influence unconsciously consumers' judgement and behaviour leading to higher donation (Peck and Wiggins 2006; Peck and Johnson 2011).

Despite the focus of previous literature on texture, other dimensions of tactile stimulation are at stake when consumers evaluate products. For instance, the weight of the product signals its quality such that the heavier and the more positive the evaluation of the product is (Piqueras-Fiszman and Spence 2012). Moreover Ackerman et al. (2010) emphasise that the contact with a hard object—in their experiment the seat on which the buyer sits—enhances the buyer rigidity during bargaining process. Plus, temperature of an object may modify its evaluation: for instance, a sheet of paper will be perceived as more feminine if it is warm (Krishna et al. 2010).

Consequently, adding tactile cues to products tends to favour tactile interaction in consumers' behaviours and thus to handle to product. This tactile interaction, either conscious or unconscious, can have a positive or negative overall effect on product evaluation, purchase intention and so on as previously discussed. However, if texture involves higher tendency to interact with products that influences product evaluation, the latter also relies on individual preference for touching such as some consumers do not like to touch product in-store after others even though their high NFT. This is known as product contamination effect in the marketing literature, and we develop the few literatures that exist on this matter hereafter.

1.2.3.2 Product Contamination

When shopping in-store, consumers often grasp products to select and examine them without necessarily intend to purchase. As well, it is frequent to observe that, when consumers are satisfied with their product examination, they replace it on the store shelf to grab the exact same other one that is deeply folded or stored below or in the back such as it is believed to have never been handled before by other consumers (Morales and Fitzsimons 2007). This rather non-logical behaviour is frequently observed and comes to question the negative effect of touch into consumption: contamination effect relies on the fact that touch transmits others' dirtiness and that touch is the non-pure sense among all (Nemeroff and Rozin 1994).

Contamination effect is based on the contagion law that overall states "once in contact, always in contact". More precisely, the laws establish that it exists a "permanent transfer of properties from one object to another by a brief contact" (Argo et al. 2006; Rozin and Fallon 1987; Rozin et al. 1999). Thus, the contagion effect reflects the time consideration a mere touch can have on product contamination perception which can lead to disgust and product rejection even though, at first stand, the consumer would have had a positive evaluation of it (Rozin et al. 1986). Besides, contamination effect relies on two perspectives: a source and a receiver. Although the source can be perceived positively, when it is not the case the negative influence on the product touched evaluation (i.e. the receiver) tends to be stronger (Rozin and Kalat 1971). Notion of disgust (i.e. repulsive sensation that is unpleasant) is associated with a negative image (Rozin and Fallon 1987). As a consequence, when consumers have a repulsive feeling about a product or the person representing the source of touch, it leads to an implicit avoidance behaviour (Rozin et al. 1999).

Yet contagion law can also have a positive impact on consumers' behaviour even though most of marketing research so far has concentrated on negative effect that seems to be more frequent. Argo et al. (2006) establish different levels of perceived contamination. Indeed, according to the level of knowledge the consumer has about a potential preceding touch from an external source; here, another consumer, the disgust feeling will be more or less important and thus influences differently the product negative perception. Besides, two major effects are observed when the source is known or not: on the one hand, when the consumers are unable to identify previous source of interaction with the product, it tends to amplify the negative contamination effect: consumers tend to imagine negative aspect at first and sometimes to exaggerate their fit to the reality (Morales 2011). On the other hand, when consumers know the source, only sources that have been extremely well perceived and being of the opposite gender of the evaluator lead to positive influence of the contamination effect. Therefore, contamination effect is a combination of factor that can lead to either real positive or negative outcome on consumers' behaviour regarding product tactile interaction (Morales and Fitzsimons 2007). As such, texturing product needs to be thoughtfully imagined when considering the contagion law for product display. However, research in marketing is limited regarding this effect and would benefit from further investigation.

1.3   Conclusion

This chapter offered an overall introduction to the consideration of touch in consumption as a global phenomenon based on social, cultural, physical and psychological dimensions and interpretations (Fig. 1.1). We have seen that the influence of social and cultural aspect deeply leads consumption apprehension such as the contamination effect but also the way people consider and use their own haptic system. Furthermore, the chapter enables to distinguish how the tactile interaction is produced according to the source, the receiver and the environments. Specifically, the consumption environments is facing deep changes for two decades even more for the five past years where we are seeing an acceleration of technological development leading to considering even more the sense of touch unlike to what could have been thought: touch is the most important sense that will definitely enable technologies adoption and no barrier perception in virtual environments (Grundwald 2008; Parisi 2018). As such, we suggest developing in Chapter 2 the transition that touch has been through in the consumption market based on the interface mediation and its sensory implications.

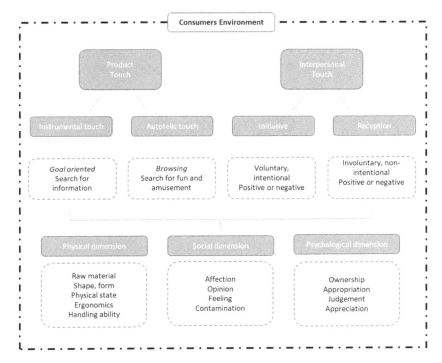

Fig. 1.1 Touch in consumption environments

References

Achrol, Ravi S., and Philip Kotler. 2012. "Frontiers of the Marketing Paradigm in the Third Millennium." *Journal of the Academy of Marketing Science* 40 (1): 35–52. https://doi.org/10.1007/s11747-011-0255-4.

Ackerman, Diane. 1990. *A Natural History of the Senses*. New York, NY: Random House.

Ackerman, Joshua M., Christopher C. Nocera, and John A. Bargh. 2010. "Incidental Haptic Sensations Influence Social Judgments and Decisions." *Science* 328 (5986): 1712–15. https://doi.org/10.1126/science.1189993.

Alba, J., C. Janiszewski, R. Lutz, A. Sawyer, and S. Wood. 1997. "Achat Interactif à Domicile: Quels Avantages Pour Les Consommateurs, Les Distributeurs et Les Producteurs Présents Sur Le Marché Électronique." *Journal of Marketing*. https://doi.org/10.1177/076737019801300306.

Andersen, Peter A., and Kenneth Leibowitz. 1978. "The Development and Nature of the Construct Touch Avoidance." *Environmental Psychology and Nonverbal Behavior* 3 (2): 89–106. https://doi.org/10.1007/BF01135607.

Argo, Jennifer J., Darren W. Dahl, and Andrea C. Morales. 2006. "Consumer Contamination: How Consumers React to Products Touched by Others." *Journal of Marketing* 70 (2): 81–94.

Barsalou, Lawrence W. 2008. "Grounded Cognition." *Annual Review of Psychology* 59 (1): 617–45. https://doi.org/10.1146/annurev.psych.59.103006.093639.

———. 2010. "Grounded Cognition: Past, Present, and Future." *Topics in Cognitive Science* 2 (4): 716–24. https://doi.org/10.1111/j.1756-8765.2010.01115.x.

Borghi, Anna M, and Diane Pecher. 2012. *Embodied and Grounded Cognition. Embodied and Grounded Cognition.* https://doi.org/10.3389/978-2-88919-013-3.

Brasel, S. Adam, and James Gips. 2014. "Tablets, Touchscreens, and Touchpads: How Varying Touch Interfaces Trigger Psychological Ownership and Endowment." *Journal of Consumer Psychology* 24 (2): 226–33. https://doi.org/10.1016/j.jcps.2013.10.003.

———. 2015. "Interface Psychology: Touchscreens Change Attribute Importance, Decision Criteria, and Behavior in Online Choice." *Cyberpsychology, Behavior, and Social Networking* 18 (9): 534–38. https://doi.org/10.1089/cyber.2014.0546.

Cascio, Carissa J., David Moore, and Francis McGlone. 2019. "Social Touch and Human Development." *Developmental Cognitive Neuroscience* 35 (March 2018): 5–11. https://doi.org/10.1016/j.dcn.2018.04.009.

Citrin, Alka Varma, Donald E. Stem, Eric R. Spangenberg, and Michael J. Clark. 2003. "Consumer Need for Tactile Input: An Internet Retailing Challenge." *Journal of Business Research* 56 (11): 915–22. https://doi.org/10.1016/S0148-2963(01)00278-8.

Coulmas, Corinna. 2012. *Métaphore Des Cinq Sens Dans l'imaginaire Occidental.* Vol. I. Paris: Les Editio.

Cummins, Shannon, James W. Peltier, John A. Schibrowsky, and Alexander Nill. 2014. "Consumer Behavior in the Online Context." Edited by Dr. Angela Hausman. *Journal of Research in Interactive Marketing* 8 (3): 169–202. https://doi.org/10.1108/JRIM-04-2013-0019.

d'Astous, Alain, and Estelle Kamau. 2010. "Consumer Product Evaluation Based on Tactile Sensory Information." *Journal of Consumer Behaviour* 9 (3): 206–13.

de Mooij, Marieke, and Geert Hofstede. 2010. "The Hofstede Model." *International Journal of Advertising* 29 (1): 85–110. https://doi.org/10.2501/S026504870920104X.

de Mooij, Marieke, Geert Hofstede, Marieke de Mooij, and Geert Hofstede. 2011. "Cross-Cultural Consumer Behavior: A Review of Research Findings." *Journal of International Consumer Marketing* 23 (June): 181–92. https://doi.org/10.1080/08961530.2011.578057.

Degeratu, Alexandru M., Arvind Rangaswamy, and Jianan Wu. 2000. "Consumer Choice Behavior in Online and Traditional Supermarkets: The Effects of Brand Name, Price, and Other Search Attributes." *International Journal of Research in Marketing* 17 (1): 55–78. https://doi.org/10.1016/S0167-8116(00)00005-7.

Dhar, Ravi, and Klaus Wertenbroch. 2000. "Consumer Choice Between Hedonic and Utilitarian Goods." *Journal of Marketing Research* 37 (1): 60–71. https://doi.org/10.1017/CBO9781107415324.004.

Ekman, Gösta, Jan Hosman, and Brita Lindström. 1965. "Roughness, Smoothness, and Preference: A Study of Quantitative Relations in Individual Subjects." *Scandinavian Journal of Psychology* 6 (4): 241–53. https://doi.org/10.1037/h0021985.

Field, Tiffany M. 1998. "Massage Therapy Effects." *The American Psychologist* 53 (12): 1270–81. https://doi.org/10.1037//0003-066X.53.12.1270.

Fuchs, Philippe, and Guillaume Moreau. 2003. *Le Traité de La Réalité Virtuelle - Fondements et Interfaces Comportementales*. Edited by Philippe Fuchs and Guillaume Moreau. Paris: Presse de.

Gallace, Alberto, and Charles Spence. 2010. "The Science of Interpersonal Touch: An Overview." *Neuroscience and Biobehavioral Reviews* 34 (2): 246–59. https://doi.org/10.1016/j.neubiorev.2008.10.004.

Giboreau, Agnès, Séverine Navarro, Pauline Faye, and Jacqueline Dumortier. 2001. "Sensory Evaluation of Automotive Fabrics." *Food Quality and Preference* 12 (5–7): 311–22. https://doi.org/10.1016/S0950-3293(01)00016-7.

Gibson, J. J. 1962. "Observations on Active Touch." *Psychological Review* 69 (6): 477–91. https://doi.org/10.1037/h0046962.

Gregory, R. L. L. 1967. "Origin of Eyes and Brains." *Nature* 213 (5074): 369–72. https://doi.org/10.1038/213369a0.

Grewen, Karen M., Bobbi J. Anderson, Susan S. Girdler, and Kathleen C. Light. 2003. "Warm Partner Contact Is Related to Lower Cardiovascular Reactivity." *Behavioral Medicine* 29 (3): 123–30. https://doi.org/10.1080/08964280309596065.

Grohmann, Bianca, Eric R. Spangenberg, and David E. Sprott. 2007. "The Influence of Tactile Input on the Evaluation of Retail Product Offerings." *Journal of Retailing* 83 (2): 237–45. https://doi.org/10.1016/j.jretai.2006.09.001.

Grundwald, Martin. 2008. *Human Haptic Perception, Basic and Applications*. Edited by Martin Grundwald. Berlin: Birkhäuser.

Guéguen, Nicolas, and Céline Jacob. 2005. "The Effect of Touch on Tipping: An Evaluation in a French Bar." *International Journal of Hospitality Management* 24 (2): 295–99. https://doi.org/10.1016/j.ijhm.2004.06.004.

Guest, Steve, Greg Essick, Jean Marc Dessirier, Kevin Blot, Kannapon Lopetcharat, and Francis McGlone. 2009. "Sensory and Affective Judgments of Skin during Inter- and Intrapersonal Touch." *Acta Psychologica* 130 (2): 115–26. https://doi.org/10.1016/j.actpsy.2008.10.007.

Heller, Morton A. 1982. "Visual and Tactual Texture-Perception—Intersensory Cooperation." *Perception & Psychophysics* 31 (4): 339–44. https://doi.org/10.3758/bf03202657.

Hertenstein, Matthew J., Julie M. Verkamp, Alyssa M. Kerestes, and Rachel M. Holmes. 2006. "The Communicative Functions of Touch in Humans, Nonhuman Primates, and Rats: A Review and Synthesis of the Empirical Research." *Genetic, Social, and General Psychology Monographs* 132 (1): 5–94. https://doi.org/10.3200/MONO.132.1.5-94.

Heslin, Richard, Tuan D. Nguyen, and Michele L. Nguyen. 1983. "Meaning of Touch: The Case of Touch from a Stranger or Same Sex Person." *Journal of Nonverbal Behavior* 7 (3): 147–57. https://doi.org/10.1007/BF00986945.

Hirschman, Elizabeth C., and Morris B Holbrook. 1982. "Hedonic Consumption: Emerging Concepts, Methods and Propositions." *Journal of Marketing* 46 (3): 92–101. https://doi.org/10.2307/1251707.

Hofstede, Geert. 1983. "National Cultures in Four Dimensions: A Research-Based Theory of Cultural Differences Among Nations." *International Studies of Management & Organization* 13 (1–2): 46–74. https://doi.org/10.1080/00208825.1983.11656358.

Holbrook, Morris B., and Elizabeth C. Hirschman. 1982. "The Experiential Aspects of Consumption: Consumer Fantasies, Feelings, and Fun." *Journal of Consumer Research* 9 (2): 132–41.

Hornik, Jacob. 1992. "Effects of Physical Contact on Customers' Shopping Time and Behavior." *Marketing Letters* 3 (1): 49–55. http://link.springer.com/article/10.1007/BF00994080.

Jin, Seung-A. Annie. 2011. "The Impact of 3D Virtual Haptics in Marketing." *Psychology and Marketing* 28 (3): 240–55. https://doi.org/10.1002/mar.20390.

Jütte, R. 2008. "Haptic Perception: A Historical Approach." In *Human Haptic Perception, Basics and Applications*, edited by Martin Grundwald. Berlin: Birkhäuser.

Klatzky, Roberta L., and Joann Peck. 2012. "Please Touch: Object Properties That Invite Touch." *IEEE Transactions on Haptics* 5 (2): 139–47. https://doi.org/10.1109/TOH.2011.54.

Klatzky, Roberta L., and Susan J. Lederman. 1993. "Toward a Computational Model of Constraint-Driven Exploration and Haptic Object Identification." *Perception* 22: 597–621.

Klatzky, Roberta L., Susan J. Lederman, and Catherine Reed. 1987. "There's More to Touch than Meets the Eye: The Salience of Object Attributes for Haptics with and without Vision." *Journal of Experimental Psychology: General* 116 (4): 356–69.

Klatzky, Roberta L., Susan J. Lederman, and D. E Matula. 1991. "Imagined Haptic Exploration in Judgments of Object Properties." *Journal of Experimental Psychology: Learning, Memory, and Cognition* 17 (2): 314–22.

———. 1993. "Haptic Exploration in the Presence of Vision." *Journal of Experimental Psychology: Human Perception and Performance* 19 (4): 726–43.

Klatzky, Roberta L., Susan J. Lederman, and Victoria A. Metzger. 1985. "Identifying Objects by Touch: An 'Expert System'." *Perception & Psychophysics* 37 (4): 299–302. https://doi.org/10.3758/BF03211351.

Krishna, Aradhna. 2006. "Interaction of Senses: The Effect of Vision versus Touch on the Elongation Bias." *Journal of Consumer Research* 32 (4): 557–66.

———. 2010. *Sensory Marketing: Research on the Sensuality of Products*. New York, NY: Routledge. https://doi.org/10.4324/9780203892060.

———. 2012. "An Integrative Review of Sensory Marketing: Engaging the Senses to Affect Perception, Judgment and Behavior." *Journal of Consumer Psychology* 22 (3): 332–51. https://doi.org/10.1016/j.jcps.2011.08.003.

Krishna, Aradhna, and Maureen Morrin. 2008. "Does Touch Affect Taste? The Perceptual Transfer of Product Container Haptic Cues." *Journal of Consumer Research* 34 (6): 807–18. https://doi.org/10.1086/523286.

Krishna, Aradhna, and Norbert Schwarz. 2014. "Sensory Marketing, Embodiment, and Grounded Cognition: A Review and Introduction." *Journal of Consumer Psychology* 24 (2): 159–68. https://doi.org/10.1016/j.jcps.2013.12.006.

Krishna, Aradhna, Ryan S. Elder, and Cindy Caldara. 2010. "Feminine to Smell but Masculine to Touch? Multisensory Congruence and Its Effect on the Aesthetic Experience☆." *Journal of Consumer Psychology* 20 (4): 410–18. https://doi.org/10.1016/j.jcps.2010.06.010.

Lal, R., and M. Sarvary. 1999. "When and How Is the Internet Likely to Decrease Price Competition?" *Marketing Science* 18 (4): 485–503. https://doi.org/10.1287/mksc.18.4.485.

Le Petit Larousse Illustré. 2010. *Larousse Editions.* ISBN 2035840783.

Lederman, Susan J., and Roberta L. Klatzky. 1987. "Hand Movements: A Window into Haptic Object Recognition." *Cognitive Psychology* 19 (3): 342–68. https://doi.org/10.1016/0010-0285(87)90008-9.

Lederman, S. J., and R. L. Klatzky. 2009. "Haptic Perception: A Tutorial." *Attention, Perception & Psychophysics* 71 (7): 1439–59. https://doi.org/10.3758/APP.71.7.1439.

Lindstrom, Martin. 2005. "Broad Sensory Branding." *Journal of Product & Brand Management* 14 (2): 84–87. https://doi.org/10.1108/10610420510592554.

Marlow, N., and C. V. Jansson-Boyd. 2011. "To Touch or Not to Touch; That Is the Question. Should Consumers Always Be Encouraged to Touch Products, and Does It Always Alter Product Perception?" *Psychology & Marketing* 28 (3): 256–66.

Martin, Brett A. S. 2012. "A Stranger's Touch: Effects of Accidental Interpersonal Touch on Consumer Evaluations and Shopping Time." *Journal of Consumer Research* 39 (1): 174–84. https://doi.org/10.1086/662038.

McCabe, Deborah Brown, and Stephen M. Nowlis. 2003. "The Effect of Examining Actual Products or Product Descriptions on Consumer Preference." *Journal of Consumer Psychology* 13 (4): 431–39. https://doi.org/10.1207/S15327663JCP1304_10.

Montagu, Ashley. 1971. *Touching: The Human Significance of the Skin.* New York, NY: Columbia U.

Morales, Andrea C. 2011. "Understanding the Role of Incidental Touch in Consumer Behavior." In *Sensory Marketing Research on the Sensuality of Products*, edited by Aradhna Krishna, 14.

Morales, Andrea C., and Gavan J. Fitzsimons. 2007. "Product Contagion: Changing Consumer Evaluations Through Physical Contact with 'Disgusting' Products." *Journal of Marketing Research* 44 (2): 272–83. https://doi.org/10.1509/jmkr.44.2.272.

Nemeroff, C., and P. Rozin. 1994. "The Contagion Concept in Adult Thinking in the United States: Transmission of Germs and of Interpersonal

Influence." *Ethos* 22 (2): 158–86. http://onlinelibrary.wiley.com/doi/10.1525/eth.1994.22.2.02a00020/full.

Nguyen, Tuan, Richard Heslin, and Michele L Nguyen. 1975. "The Meanings of Touch: Sex Differences." *Journal of Communication* 25 (3): 92–103. https://doi.org/10.1111/j.1460-2466.1975.tb00610.x.

Okamoto, Shogo, Hikaru Nagano, and Yoji Yamada. 2013. "Psychophysical Dimensions of Tactile Perception of Textures." *IEEE Transactions on Haptics* 6 (1): 81–93.

Parisi, David. 2018. *Archaeologies of Touch: Interfacing with Haptics from Electricity to Computing*. University of Minnesota Press.

Patterson, Miles L., Jack L. Powell, and Mary G. Lenihan. 1986. "Touch, Compliance, and Interpersonal Affect." *Journal of Nonverbal Behavior* 10 (1): 41–50. https://doi.org/10.1007/BF00987204.

Peck, Joann, and T. L. Childers. 2003a. "Individual Differences in Haptic Information Processing: The 'Need for Touch' Scale." *Journal of Consumer Research* 30 (3): 430–43.

———. 2003b. "To Have and to Hold: The Influence of Haptic Information on Product Judgments." *Journal of Marketing* 67 (2): 35–48.

Peck, Joann, and Terry L. Childers. 2006. "If I Touch It I Have to Have It: Individual and Environmental Influences on Impulse Purchasing." *Journal of Business Research* 59 (6): 765–69.

Peck, Joann, and Suzanne B. Shu. 2009. "The Effect of Mere Touch on Perceived Ownership." *Journal of Consumer Research* 36 (3): 434–47. https://doi.org/10.1086/598614.

Peck, Joann, and Jennifer Wiggins. 2006. "It Just Feels Good: Customers' Affective Response to Touch and Its Influence on Persuasion." *Journal of Marketing* 70 (October): 56–69.

Peck, Joann, and J. Wiggins Johnson. 2011. "Autotelic Need for Touch, Haptics, and Persuasion: The Role of Involvement." *Psychology & Marketing* 28 (3): 222–39. https://doi.org/10.1002/mar.

Penfield, WIilder, and Edwin Boldrey. 1937. "Somatic Motor and Sensory Representation in the Cerebral Cortex of Man as Studied by Electrical Stimulation." *Brain* 60 (4): 389–443. https://doi.org/10.1093/brain/60.4.389.

Picard, Delphine, Catherine Dacremont, Dominique Valentin, and Agnès Giboreau. 2003. "Perceptual Dimensions of Tactile Textures." *Acta Psychologica* 114 (2): 165–84. https://doi.org/10.1016/j.actpsy.2003.08.001.

Piqueras-Fiszman, Betina, and Charles Spence. 2012. "The Influence of the Feel of Product Packaging on the Perception of the Oral-Somatosensory

Texture of Food." *Food Quality and Preference* 26 (1): 67–73. https://doi.org/10.1016/j.foodqual.2012.04.002.

Rahman, Osmud. 2012. "The Influence of Visual and Tactile Inputs on Denim Jeans Evaluation." *International Journal of Design* 6 (1): 11–24.

Reite, M. 1990. "Touch, Attachment, and Health: Is There a Relationship." In *Touch: The Foundation of Experience*, edited by K. E. Barnar, 195–225. Madison: CT: International Universities Press.

Remland, Martin S., Tricia S. Jones, and Heidi Brinkman. 1995. "Interpersonal Distance, Body Orientation, and Touch: Effects of Culture, Gender, and Age." *The Journal of Social Psychology* 135 (3): 281–97. https://doi.org/10.1080/00224545.1995.9713958.

Révész, Gera. 1950. *Psychology and Art of the Blind*. London: Longmans G.

Rozin, Paul, and April E. Fallon. 1987. "A Perspective on Disgust." *Psychological Review* 94 (1): 23–41. https://doi.org/10.1037/0033-295X.94.1.23.

Rozin, Paul, Jonathan Haidt, and Clark R. McCauley. 1999. "Disgust: The Body and Soul Emotion." In *Handbook of Cognition and Emotion*, edited by T. Dalgleish and M. Power, 429–45. Chichester: Wiley. http://psycnet.apa.org/psycinfo/1999-04021-021.

Rozin, Paul, and James W. Kalat. 1971. "Specific Hungers and Poison Avoidance as Adaptive Specializations of Learning." *Psychological Review* 78 (6): 459–86. https://doi.org/10.1037/h0031878.

Rozin, Paul, Linda Millman, and Carol Nemeroff. 1986. "Operation of the Laws of Sympathetic Magic in Disgust and Other Domains." *Journal of Personality and Social Psychology* 50 (4): 703–12. https://doi.org/10.1037/0022-3514.50.4.703.

Serino, Andrea, and Patrick Haggard. 2010. "Touch and the Body." *Neuroscience and Biobehavioral Reviews* 34 (2): 224–36. https://doi.org/10.1016/j.neubiorev.2009.04.004.

Shu, Suzanne B., and Joann Peck. 2011. "Psychological Ownership and Affective Reaction: Emotional Attachment Process Variables and the Endowment Effect." *Journal of Consumer Psychology* 21 (4): 439–52. https://doi.org/10.1016/j.jcps.2011.01.002.

Skedung, Lisa, Katrin Danerlöv, Ulf Olofsson, Carl Michael Johannesson, Maiju Aikala, John Kettle, Martin Arvidsson, Birgitta Berglund, and Mark W. Rutland. 2011. "Tactile Perception: Finger Friction, Surface Roughness and Perceived Coarseness." *Tribology International* 44 (5): 505–12.

Smith, Tom. 2009. "The Social Media Revolution." *International Journal of Market Research* 51 (4): 559–61. https://doi.org/10.2501/S1470785309200773.

Soufflet, Ivanne, Maurice Calonnier, and Catherine Dacremont. 2004. "A Comparison Between Industrial Experts' and Novices' Haptic Perceptual Organization: A Tool to Identify Descriptors of the Handle of Fabrics." *Food Quality and Preference* 15 (7–8 SPEC.ISS.): 689–99. https://doi.org/10.1016/j.foodqual.2004.03.005.

Streicher, Mathias C., and Zachary Estes. 2015. "Touch and Go: Merely Grasping a Product Facilitates Brand Perception and Choice." *Applied Cognitive Psychology* 29 (3). https://doi.org/10.1002/acp.3109.

———. 2016. "Multisensory Interaction in Product Choice: Grasping a Product Affects Choice of Other Seen Products." *Journal of Consumer Psychology* 26 (4). https://doi.org/10.1016/j.jcps.2016.01.001.

Webb, Andrea, and Joann Peck. 2015. "Individual Differences in Interpersonal Touch: On the Development, Validation, and Use of the 'Comfort with Interpersonal Touch' (CIT) Scale." *Journal of Consumer Psychology* 25 (1): 60–77.

Whitcher, Sheryle J., and Jeffrey D. Fisher. 1979. "Multidimensional Reaction to Therapeutic Touch in a Hospital Setting." *Journal of Personality and Social Psychology* 37 (1): 87–96.

Willis, Frank N., and Helen K. Hamm. 1980. "The Use of Interpersonal Touch in Securing Compliance." *Journal of Nonverbal Behavior* 5 (1): 49–55. https://doi.org/10.1007/BF00987054.

Willis, Frank N., and Leon F. Briggs. 1992. "Relationship and Touch in Public Settings." *Journal of Nonverbal Behavior* 16 (1): 55–63. https://doi.org/10.1007/BF00986879.

Yazdanparast, Atefeh, and Nancy Spears. 2012. "Need for Touch and Information Processing Strategies: An Empirical Examination." *Journal of Consumer Behaviour* 11 (5): 415–21. https://doi.org/10.1002/cb.1393.

———. 2013. "Can Consumers Forgo the Need to Touch Products? An Investigation of Nonhaptic Situational Factors in an Online Context." *Psychology & Marketing* 30 (1): 46–61. https://doi.org/10.1002/mar.20588.

Yoshida. 1968. "Dimensions of Tactual Impressions." *Japanese Psychological Research* 10 (3): 123–37.

Zwaan, Rolf A. 1999. "Embodied Cognition, Perceptual Symbols, and Situation Models." *Discourse Processes* 28 (1): 81–88. https://doi.org/10.1080/01638539909545070.

2

Touching Without Touching: The Paradox of the Digital Age

Abstract This chapter aims to show the evolution between the different environments in which consumers and products constantly interact: Internet and associated technologies have enabled new ways of interactions through mobile devices such as consumers tend to proceed to purchase without even touching products. Many researches from the 90s along with the development of the Internet have raised the question of the inability to touch in these upcoming environments unless that haptic feedback would be further integrated for consumption usage. Accordingly, this chapter exposes the new consumer journeys through digital interfaces and reviews part of the literature on virtual environments and afferents notions that are virtual and augmented reality to position the new consumers' experience through interfaces as well as the change in consumption habits.

Keywords Digital · Internet · Interfaces · Mediated environments · Consumer journey

This chapter aims to show the evolution between the different environments in which consumers and products constantly interact: Internet and associated technologies have enabled new ways of interactions through mobile devices such as consumers tend to proceed to purchase without even touching products. Many researches from the 90s along with the development of the Internet have raised the question of the inability to touch in these upcoming environments unless that haptic feedback would be further integrated for consumption usage. Accordingly, this chapter exposes the new consumer journeys through digital interfaces and reviews part of the literature on virtual environments and afferents notions that are virtual and augmented reality to position the new consumers' experience through interfaces as well as the change in consumption habits.

2.1 Internet Environment: Evolution of Consumers' Experience with Products

Touching through the interface is a challenge that marketers have overcome by different ways based on the evolution of technologies to offer new consumers experiences but is now about to change radically with the introduction of touch into virtual consumption environments (Parisi 2014). First approaches of interactive home shopping—corresponding to the Internet shopping—early considered the problematic that consumers would face for purchasing, in particular from a logistic and tactual problematic as earlier identify for mail-order selling (Alba et al. 1997a, b; Katz and Aspden 1997). For instance, purchasing in store consisted to go to the store while nowadays it is possible to purchase through a mobile device (i.e. computer, smartphone, tablets) over the world and to either collect it at the store or receive it at home (Dholakia et al. 2005; Watson et al. 2015; Shankar et al. 2010). Yet conclusions from this stream of research lead to consider the great opportunities that is Internet according to the development of technologies for enhancing the online experience with products. In line with it, Cummins et al. (2014) consider three phases that deeply influenced the development of online consumption: incubation (1993–2004), expansion (2005–2008) and explosion (2009–2012). These three phases also correspond to the chronological development and progress in technologies enabling the access to online environments but also to new types of interaction—from only reading to socially exchange and connect to others. Thus, in less than a decade, by 2007, Internet became rooted into everyone's knowledge even though not necessarily in everyone's habits yet (Hung and Li 2007; Hoffman et al. 2004; Hoffman and Novak 1996). However, a decade later, in 2019, Internet is considered as a routine and deeply rules our interactions with the world, objects and others as, for instance, the VivaTech[1] world fair demonstrate it. Indeed, consumers interact and purchase in both environments, off- and online, daily from the moment they get up to the moment they go to sleep, according to their instant need and to the perceived benefits of each channels (e.g. time consuming, delivery, information, etc.) (Bèzes 2012; Keen et al. 2004). Therefore, the time to consider the tangibility as a real potential between people and products over the Internet has come after having considered the dematerialised information (i.e. websites) (Chen et al. 2002; Hsu et al. 2012) and interaction with people (i.e. social media) (Hennig-Thurau et al. 2013; Yadav et al. 2013). Several strategies have been developed to enhance so-called virtual reality—VR—with digital devices from the use of 3D images on screens to technologies dedicated to a complete sensory stimulation.

2.1.1 New Consumers' Experience: Online Image Interactivity

Websites or webpages represent the physical realities of the online environment within which all types of interactions occur between people to people and people to products (Chen et al. 2010; Milgram et al. 1994). As a consequence, images are at the core of online, augmented and virtual realities. Within these environments, companies search for compensating the absence of direct interactions with the store in using images. Thus, the online "store" needs to provide the same or adequate experience for the consumers with products and the brand to make it flowing and pleasant as in physical location (Chen et al. 2010; Hsu et al. 2012). Therefore, online store provides textual and visual information to facilitate consumers' decision-making, and this information is adapted to

---

[1] https://vivatechnology.com/.

each online customer since marketers' apprehension of online consumers' behaviour enables clearer information, faster services and more efficient product offer in general (Grewal et al. 2017). Despite this information increase, the lack of product tangibility induces consumer distrust managers have to cope with. For almost two decades, numerous researches have also investigated ways to offer more trustful environments for consumers to enable them to purchase safely online (Gefen et al. 2003; Heijden et al. 2003; McCole et al. 2010; Schlosser et al. 2006).

To better understand consumers' use of Internet and its new technologies, models have largely relied on the Technology Acceptance Model (TAM) (Davis 1986, 1989). Overall, the TAM predicts that the easier and the more useful a technology is perceived, the less risky it is, and thus, consumers can proceed to purchase through it (Davis 1989; Ha and Stoel 2009; Vijayasarathy 2004). However, the TAM model has largely been discussed over the literature and we invite the reader that is interested to further read on the topic to observe the divergent theoretical issues since it is out of the scope of the current discussion here (Schepers and Wetzels 2007; Venkatesh et al. 2012; Dishaw and Strong 1999; Bagozzi 2007; Bagozzi and Lee 1999; Davis et al. 1989, 1992). Thus, thanks to the provided efforts to predict online consumers' behaviour, it is clear today that consumers are familiar with online environments which lead companies to further concentrate on the full experience they provide to their customers to compensate with the absence of physical interaction, in particular by touching (Childers et al. 2001).

To overcome the barrier of intangibility, image use has not to be restricted to a simple static information use. Literature emphasises the use of online image interactivity to create more vivid experiences in online environments that comes closer to the physical realities in terms of stimulation of the senses (Noort et al. 2012; Coyle and Thorson 2001; Varadarajan et al. 2010). Interactivity corresponds to the level of modification and manipulation over the online content a consumer has, while vividness is the illusion of proximity, either physical, time-distant or emotional (Fuchs and Moreau 2006). From a technological perspective, vividness is the relative capacity of the interface to procure a rich sensory experience within the online environment (Steuer 1992, p. 10). Vividness is further composed of the length (number of senses stimulated) and the depth (closeness to the human senses system). Thus, interactivity and vividness are two main characteristics of the online product experience that represent the closest way to overcome the barrier of intangibility to better immerse the consumers in the online environment from a sensory perspective (Hoffman and Novak 1996). Interestingly, during interviews, researchers noticed that some consumers had difficulties to "get out" of the virtual shopping environment during an immersive experience due to the higher sensory stimulation (Poncin and Garnier 2010). Furthermore, online consumers' approach of products depends on whether the website is static or dynamic—i.e. with 3D images or virtual try-on settings (Kim and Forsythe 2008a, b). The latter enables to stimulate more senses by allowing movements of the product directed by the hand and making the product to move (i.e. rotate, slide, etc.), which in turn induces higher level of mental representations retrieving grounded sensations (Barsalou 2010; Krishna and Schwarz 2014). As a consequence, the dynamism of the online environment leads to the mobilisation of the haptic system, beyond other sensory cues, that generates a more natural interaction with the online product, which thus comes closer to the physical interaction (Kock 2004, 2005; Overmars and Poels 2015). Using dynamic imagery and technologies enabling online interactivity between the consumer and the product induces a greater ability to project and mentally imagine the product and its use in physical conditions (Li et al. 2001, 2002; Schlosser 2003; Schlosser et al. 2006). Thus, the online experience becomes richer in sensory load, and this effect is particularly true for products that are geometrical or mechanical (Li et al. 2003).

In line with it, Jiang and Benbasat (2004) introduced the concept of virtual product experience that underlines the role of perceived control and diagnostic during online navigation. They define virtual product experience as being a *web shopping experiences that allow consumers to interact with and try products* via *web interfaces* (Jiang and Benbasat 2004, 2007). They demonstrate that the more the consumer feels in control of the online product visualisation the more she/he can determine the product characteristics and understand it, which holds true for various dynamic product presentation formats (i.e. videos, virtual product presentation, etc.). More recently, Choi and Taylor (2014) investigated the role of need for touch into the online product presentation format effect (i.e. dynamic vs. static) and considered as well the type of product (i.e. material or geometrical). Their results demonstrate the superiority of dynamic images over the static in all cases. However, the authors show that 3D images work better for product with geometrical properties and that only lower NFT profiles tend to revisit the websites, which is explained by the authors with a frustration effect of the inability to really touch the product for high NFT profiles.

Consequently, Internet has brought new consumers' product experiences, beyond the physical environment, that technologies constantly improve to allow consumers to act "as if" they were able to interact with the product physically (Schlosser 2006). In this online environment, the sense of sight is actively stimulated via images to compensate for the lack of other sense stimulations. Thus, Internet has shaped a new consumption environment where interactions translate from different realities (Milgram et al. 1994) and create new forms of human to machine relationships, especially from the sensory perspective, where the haptic system struggle to be represented (Micu et al. 2011; Sreelakshmi and Subash 2017). These new forms of interactions are commonly labelled human–machine interaction or computer-mediated interactions. For this reason, interfaces have an important role to play to retrieve and extend the human haptic sensations in novels environments that, for some, we still ignore their coming existence (Parisi 2014; Grundwald 2008; Parisi 2008; Parisi et al. 2017).

2.1.2 Mediated Environments: Human–Machine Interactions

The Davos Conference 2016,[2] on the horizon 2020, put the Internet forward as a major theme, being the fourth industrial revolution, to invite companies and engineers to re-think technologies and make it more flowing and more natural for users and mass market. Indeed, along

---

[2]https://www.weforum.org/events/world-economic-forum-annual-meeting-2016/.

the time and technical investments, physical and virtual consumers' environments become seamless and begin to merge (Micu et al. 2011), leading to richer and more complex consumption experiences (Bridges and Florsheim 2008) and to new sensory perception pathways (Citrin et al. 2003; Grohmann et al. 2007; Kerrebroeck et al. 2017). Notably, previous research findings underline that the limited product sensory experience through the interface reduces purchase intention over the Internet (Grewal et al. 2004; Keen et al. 2004).

Undoubtedly, the interface brings new parameters for consumption that create new relationships between the consumers, the medium and the firm (Yadav and Pavlou 2014). For instance, today's typical consumption path is composed of multiple interactions between the store and one or several devices—often a smartphone, tablets or computer but also smartwatch, etc. before proceeding to purchase (Collin-Lachaud and Vanheems 2016). Hence, consumers have integrated the interface into their relational approach to the products and the store, as a means to access to a wide range of services and shopping experiences (Merle et al. 2012; Coyle and Thorson 2001). However, these new relationships imply different sensory load related to the shopping environment such as the consumers stands in a different location than the products, which is accessed with the device (Milgram et al. 1994).

Accordingly, the market has recently welcomed new type of human–machine interaction technology with new level of sensory stimulation to consider: the voice input. In addition to current tactile dominance in mobile devices, voice interaction enables to exchange, search and purchase with only vocal commands—e.g. Alexa, Hound or Cortana (McLean and Osei-Frimpong 2019; Pagani et al. 2019). This evolution is in line with the integration of the senses into the dematerialisation process that is considered to reduce the technological mediation (Steuer 1992). Therefore, incorporating more senses into the relationship with interfaces comes closer to Heilig's (i.e. Sensorama) and Sutherland' vision for virtual environments that should stimulate all the senses (Sutherland 1965). Besides, according to Kock (2004, 2005), the closer the indirect online experience is to the direct face-to-face one, the more natural the mediated experience. From a haptic perspective, the more the interfaces stimulate the tactile system, and those tactile signals relate to the product

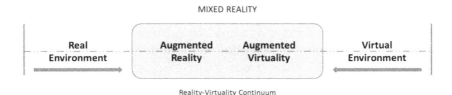

Fig. 2.1 Continuum of mixed reality (Adapted from Milgram et al. 1994)

characteristics, the more consumers are likely to understand the product through their diagnostic touch or to simply rely on their tactile sense for enjoying product touch. However, practices in business and research have not come to these results so far (Overmars and Poels 2015; Sreelakshmi and Subash 2017; Burke 1997, 2002, 2009). Indeed, the integration of more senses to the online environment leads to consider the way to define consumption environments and consumers' experience. To do so, it is possible to relate to the continuum of mixed reality suggested by Milgram et al. (1994) to delineate the consumers and products interactions and, accordingly, provide the adequate sensory stimulation and product experience (Fig. 2.1). With Internet, goods and people have been moving through different environments that go from the physical and tangible reality—i.e. where people interact directly with products and results of the interactions occur in this same environment—to the virtual environment—i.e. where people and products are projected into an intangible reality and for which interactions result into intangible outcomes as well. In between these two realities are located the augmented reality and augmented virtuality that are respectively referred based on the location of the people, the products and the actions' outcomes. More precisely, when the outcomes of an action through an interface is visible in the virtual environment, it is considered as augmented virtuality while when the outcomes are visible through digital visualisation in the physical environment, it is considered as augmented reality.

Until now, the definition of Milgram et al. (1994) has been little challenged and recent propositions are still in need of proof besides the numerous and wrong use of the term "virtual reality" in the literature and marketing business area (Kardong-Edgren et al. 2019; Steuer 1992; Flavián et al. 2019). Indeed, whether we consider computer sciences, psychology or marketing for defining the realities, the term of "virtual reality" is often misleading, especially in social sciences and marketing (Biocca 1992; Fox et al. 2009). From a marketing perspective, a limited amount of research has investigated the virtual reality definition and its implications for consumers understanding, yet numerous research has employed virtual reality settings to search for understanding consumers' behaviour in these mixed environments (Martínez-Navarro et al. 2019; Kannan and Li 2017; Shankar et al. 2010; Hofacker 2012). The result is that we still need further understanding of what the new environments are and how people act within each and all of them. Nevertheless, definitions exist in other fields and we propose to review few definitions that should be helpful for considering and understanding the virtual consumption environment before moving on to the next chapter on the haptic integration into interfaces.

"Virtual Reality" is a term coined by Jaron Lanier in the USA in the 80s that became largely diffused and used among mass-market people and business, even though not always accurately (Fuchs and Moreau 2006). Nowadays, the term of VR is more and more discussed as the phase of exciting novelty and fantasy imagination is over and that reality of business and research has come to specify furthermore the technicity of it, its applications and its influence on human behaviour (Kardong-Edgren et al. 2019). In this way, Fuchs and Moreau (2006) gather in their "Traité de la Réalité Virtuelle" a consensus on the definition of VR and state that immersion and interaction are among the wildest accepted dimensions. Therefore, they introduced the following scientific and technical definition: "*virtual reality is a scientific and technical domain that exploits computer sciences and behavioural interfaces to simulate in virtual environments 3D entities' behaviours, which are in real-time interaction between each other or with external users that are in pseudo-natural immersion through the intermediary of sensory-motors channels*" (p. 7). Here, virtual environments consider the use of a technology that enables anyone to project and be projected into a new dimension that allows fluid and continuous interaction thanks to the sensory stimulation. Particularly, their definition incorporates the label of *virtual environments* that Ellis (1991) proposed to consider to describe the virtualisation of the interactions and location of people and objects. Virtual environments also integrate the notion of immersion and interaction, which is different from the image interactivity in online website. According to Fuchs and Moreau (2006), consumers are not only passively moving through the environments but are actively acting in the immersive environments. Immersion is a multidisciplinary concept subdivided between the technological and psychological dimensions, allowing consumers to either transfer his or her mind and body into the physical experience (i.e. the book dilemma) (Biocca 2003) or virtual one (i.e. Second Life) (Kaplan and Haenlein 2009). From the technological perspective, it consists in the device capacity to develop an immersive environment for the human–machine relationship. This capacity relies on the stimulations of the five senses (i.e. if we consider the occidental approach of the senses) with the visual, haptic, auditory, olfactory and gustatory systems (Parisi 2018; Grundwald 2008). Thus, the more senses are stimulated, the more consumers feel immersed in the experience with the product, whether it is mediated or not. The immersive approach goes in line with the media richness theory proposed by Kock (2004, 2005) that questions the role of the interface as a communication medium allowing natural human interactions. In marketing, immersive experiences have shown the capacity of consumers to feel deeply involved and to forget about their actual reality (Poncin and Garnier 2010). From the psychological perspective, immersion is the *"inclusive, extensive, surrounding and vivid illusions of reality to the senses of human participant"* (Slater and Wilbur 1997). In their definitions, (1) *inclusive* relates the extent to which physical reality is shut down, (2) *extensive* is the number of senses solicited, (3) *surrounding* is the ability to provide a panoramic visual perception and (4) *vivid* the richness and fidelity of the sensory stimulation as previously introduced. In line with it, Li et al. (2003) define the virtual experience as psychological and emotional states a consumer lives through while interacting with products in online environment. This psychological state is inherent to computer-mediated environments and has also been reported with the theory of flow (Hoffman and Novak 1996; Csíkszentmihály 1997). However, this theory is still under development due to the numerous constructs and its broadness (Hoffman and Novak 2009). For that reason, we won't develop further the afferent theory since immersion is much more considered in both computer sciences and social sciences.

In parallel, interaction is the second concept to be considered as necessary for experiencing virtual environments. Interaction is the mutual influences between the user and the computer through sensory-, motor- and interactive-based interfaces (Sternberger 2006). It is also defined as the extent to which a user can participate in the virtual environment by modifying the shape and content of the mediated environment in real-time conditions (Steuer 1992). Interaction is often considered as indispensable for virtual reality without which consumers would not be able to transpose himself or herself into the virtual environment. It also tends to reinforce the immersive states of consumers, and thus, the overall experience depends on the type of interfaces. In line with it, computer sciences classify interfaces according to the navigation, selection, manipulation and control characteristics that enable similar interaction than in physical environments with the same products (Hand 1997). These characteristics correspond to the consumers need to detect products or locate himself/herself, choose and select, apprehend products and control the environment. In Table 2.1, we show that interfaces mechanism as the mouse, computer pad or touchscreens devices as smartphone and tablets stimulate similarly the haptic system even though in different manners, with different tactile cues.

Besides, on a close perspective to immersion and interaction, academic literature also considers the concepts of presence and telepresence to define VR without technological grounds, although the concept of *presence* itself tend to gain more success (Lee 2004; Bouvier 2008) (Table 2.2). In a nutshell, presence is psychological and physical states of a person within an environment where she/he has the feeling of *being here*. This term is favoured by Lee (2004) since it represents a non-technological approach of the sensations perceived in both environments—i.e. physical and virtual—and the denomination allows to have a transdisciplinary discussion since it is a perceptual phenomenon based on senses' stimulation. Moreover, the concept of *presence* shows the psychological dimension that computer mediation creates. For instance, the *presence* can concern the feeling of interacting in real-time sensations with the product over the Internet while it can also represent the feeling of being with the people one is talking with through a video call-conference.

Table 2.1 Interface haptic stimulation

Interface	Navigation	Selection	Manipulation	Control	Haptic stimulation
Mouse	Hand palm and fingers	Click	Continuous click pressure and slide movement	Visual and instant click	Cutaneous, pressure and movement
Computer Pad	Fingers	Double tap	Double tap and continuous touch pressure movement	Visual and double tap	Cutaneous, pressure and movement
Digital Tablet	Fingers	Double tap	Slide movement	Visual and tactile	Cutaneous, pressure and movement
Smartphone	Hand palm and fingers	Double tap	Slide movement	Visual and tactile	Cutaneous, pressure and movement

2 Touching Without Touching: The Paradox of the Digital Age

Table 2.2 Presence and telepresence definitions

Presence		Telepresence	
Authors	Definitions	Authors	Definitions
Witmer and Singer (1998)	"The subjective experience of being in one place or environment, even when one is physically situated in another"	Reeves (1991)	"Being there" to explain viewers' experience of moving into televised environments
Slater and Usoh (1994)	"The psychological sense of "being there" in the environment based on the technologically founded immersive base"	Slater and Usoh (1993)	"Suspension of disbelief that they [users of virtual reality systems] are in a world other than where their real bodies are located" (p. 222)
Gibson (1978)	"The sense of being in an environment"	Rheingold (1991)	"Form of out-of-the-body experience" (p. 256)
Steuer (1992)	"Presence refers to the natural perception of an environment"	Steuer (1992)	"The experience of presence in an environment by means of a communication medium"/"telepresence" refers to the mediated perception of an environment
Sheridan (1992)	"Virtual presence" is the term coined to refer to the presence caused by technologies	Sheridan (1992)	"Feeling like you are actually there at the remote site of operation" (p. 120)

(continued)

Table 2.2 (continued)

Presence		Telepresence	
Authors	Definitions	Authors	Definitions
Zahorik and Jenison (1998)	"Presence is tantamount to successfully supported action in the environment"	Schloerb (1995)	"Telepresence occurs when a user perceives that he or she is physically present in a remote environment"
Lombard and Ditton (2001)	"The perceptual illusion of nonmediation"	McLellan (1996)	"Feeling of being in a location other than where you actually are"
Lee (2004)	"A psychological state in which the virtuality of experience is unnoticed"	Minsky (1980)	"Emphasize the possibility that human operators could feel the sense of being physically transported to a remote work space via teleoperating systems"

De facto, the computer mediation generates the necessity, through the different environments, to consider the psychological distance between the actors, and that the interface becomes the heart of the experience since it enables the entire real-time interaction and immersion. As a result, the interface is the physical representation of the mediation effect between the different environments within which consumption occurs where all the senses need to be stimulated as for experiences in physical environments (Biocca 1992).

2.2 Impact of Mediated Environments on Consumers' Product Perception

As introduced in the first section, interaction and immersion represent essential features of the online environment for enabling consumers to obtain a pleasant and complete experience with products. In particular, the interface represents the unique link between the brand, the product and the consumers in the virtual environment. As such, the level of interactivity is critical to convince the consumer of the real "value" of its interaction with the product. To obtain such level of interactivity, and thus consumers' belief that action is real, the overall senses need to be solicited. However, the online environment remains poor for rendering a complete sensory experience of the product through the interfaces, but technologies development has enabled marketers to provide online experiences through visual and indirect haptic stimulation. We show in this second section that marketing strategies for compensating the absence of direct product touch enable to stimulates the haptic system on a visual basis.

2.2.1 Multichannel Shopping Environments: Enhancing Sensory Interactions

The development of virtual environments represents a challenge for brands and particularly from a retailing perspective (Grewal et al. 2017; Varadarajan et al. 2010). Among the most innovative approach, Amazon

Go[3] represents one of the most emblematic evolutions of the online markets and adaptation of the consumers' environments and habits for shopping products. In 2019, Amazon allows consumers with only a smartphone to move through a grocery store, pick up products and leave without using any check-out facilities but only the Amazon Go app that automatically charges and sends the bill to the consumer's account. Amazon Company even goes further to extend the consumer's experience by now providing online product testing directly on their website: consumers can try-on their make-up products virtually before proceeding to purchase through Amazon website thanks to the partnership with l'Oréal ModiFace.[4] For both experiences, either Amazon Go or virtual try-on, the consumer journey has changed as well as the sensory experience related to it. On the first case, Amazon generates a new in-store experience that enables the full sensory experience without the inconvenience of regular store that is usually time consuming and full of unwanted tactile interactions with online facilities (Argo et al. 2006). On the second case, the online full experience for purchasing a product relies on visual cues that generates sensory experiences that allow consumers to have a sense of the possible results still without the inconvenient tactile interactions.

Visual stimulation is based on image interactivity technology, which enables to overcome the absence of direct tactile interactions with the product in online configurations (2D image presentation, 3D images, videos, etc.) (Hauswiesner et al. 2013; Meng et al. 2010; Wacker and Keckeisen 2005). In comparison with other image interactive product presentation formats, virtual try-ons allow for deeper online interactivity and extend consumers' overall time spent on the website (Kim and Forsythe 2008a). As well, the higher degree of personalisation leads to better evaluation and higher purchase intention through Internet, e.g. Sephora Virtual Artist,[5] despite the lack of "realism" (Racat and Capelli 2014, 2016). Thus, personalisation is partially efficient and marketers need to consider consumers' self-body perception and congruity with the

---

[3] https://www.youtube.com/watch?v=NrmMk1Myrxc.
[4] https://mobile-ar.reality.news/news/amazon-adding-virtual-try-from-loreals-modiface-its-beauty-products-0198429/.
[5] https://sephoravirtualartist.com/landing_5.0.php?country=US&lang=en&x=&skintone=&currentModel=.

virtual try-on to ensure the benefits of visual product presentation (Merle et al. 2012). Nonetheless, when consumers dislike their body image, they tend to prefer virtual try-on settings for testing products while no effect is recorded between high and low image interactivity formats for consumers having a good self-body esteem (Yim and Park 2019). Therefore, online product interaction with virtual try-ons enables consumers to further improve their intention to purchase in online environments but also reduces product returns (Yang and Xiong 2019). Hence, virtual try-on technology is among the most dynamic and interactive possibilities for consumers to deeply interact with a product, understand its features and test it in online environments, as well as in store. Indeed, at first considered as tools for compensating the inability to touch the product online, virtual try-on tools have become real opportunities for retailers to sell off- and online with limited storage and product turn over,[6] but also to prevent unwanted tactile contamination effect. Consequently, marketers have started to understand the powerful impact of image interactivity, as the example of the cosmetic sector demonstrates, and the potential gain it can provide on products returns, consumer's satisfaction as well as sales growth (Roggeveen et al. 2015).

Another example for engaging more senses in consumption environments is the use of both online and offline retailing strategies, as Amazon Go, through Internet of Things (Verhoef et al. 2017). In this example, the connected mobile app facilitates the purchasing actions and allows consumers to spend more time with products and thus to further experience them with their senses while not even bothering with the purchasing phase. As a result, the experience engaging all the senses is at the heart of the consumption process. By using both online and physical retailing strategies, Amazon provides a new type of experience between both environments and counters the absence of product tactile interaction, as well as other senses. Hence, the evolution of technology enables radical retail and consumption transformations since nowadays consumers are deeply seamlessly connected, and considering a separation of these environments tends to make no more sense (Verhoef et al. 2017). Indeed,

---

[6] https://www.inecommerce.com/virtual-fitting-room-how-they-can-increase-sales-for-your-online-store/.

consumers search, select, test and purchase product in various environments whenever she/he decides. For instance, in search of a bike, one can look over the Internet for information about bike characteristics, comparison and determine a range of acceptable price and quality. Then, from this first introduction with the product in online environment, the consumer can go in-store and try the different products preselected online either through their smartphone, tablets or computer. Finally, the actual purchase can occur directly at the store or be proceed through online mobile app for delivery or with a pickup option. This description exhibits only one of the multiple possible interactions that Internet and online environments have created to access to the product and provides wider sensory experiences (Krishna 2012).

2.2.2 Visuo-Haptic Stimulation in Online Shopping Environments

The use of senses is necessary for reaching out consumers. Accordingly, sensory marketing aims at engaging the consumers' senses to affect their perception, judgement and behaviour (Krishna 2012). Thus, marketers should conceive product offering based on the stimulation of senses given the different environments. For the sense of touch, the challenge is thus to design products enable to induce tactile stimulation even in an online environment when the product is not touched. In this case of online product perception, the use of haptic imagery has been thoroughly investigated regarding the impact of the absence of tactile interaction with product on judgement, evaluation, confidence and purchase intention (Peck et al. 2013; Rinaldo 2008). Indeed, the role of visual cues has become dominant due to the priority given by engineers to develop current interfaces (i.e. computer, tablets and smartphone) (Parisi 2018). Yet, in the recent years, haptic stimulation has become an important issue but technical progress and investment into these type of device capacities have been slower than expected, and consequently, marketers had to adapt their sensory marketing strategies (Krishna 2012). For instance, interactive technologies allow high image definition to provide visual accurate exhibition of salient tactile cues of the product (e.g. texture)

(Wacker and Keckeisen 2005). Therefore, haptic sensory cues can be stimulated with visual tactile enhancement (Klatzky and Peck 2012). Nevertheless, texture is the unique dimension to be able to enhance haptic imagery since today technologies do not allow to evoke temperature nor load.

The visual-tactile interplay is largely demonstrated in the physical environment and its effect on consumers' cognitive, affective and conative answers (Eklund and Helmefalk 2018). Academic literature shows that this same interplay can be transferred into the online environment such as visual cues enhance products tactile cues that in turn stimulate the haptic system as if it was directly solicited. However, this stream of literature remains scarce. A research team showed that, when using image display on computer screen, consumers better perceive texture visually when the fabric is folded and coloured (i.e. other than black and white) (Xiao et al. 2016). Previously, Klatzky and Peck (2012) showed that material properties elicit touch, and thus, it is possible to define *touch-ability* properties of products for online display: the more a product image display enables consumers to perceive the material and geometrical properties of the product, the more it will trigger the haptic system and make the consumers feel tactile sensations as if it were tangible. Indeed, haptic stimulation in online environment mostly relies on the material properties of the product through notably the texture (Ferreira et al. 2013). However, Etzi and Gallace (2016) demonstrated that visual apprehension of texture leads to lower pleasant perception of texture than actual tactile stimulation: seeing a texture differs from the meaning inferred after touching the same texture.

2.3 Conclusion

As we just presented, the touch-ability of the product presented of the screen of the device depends on its visual texture that induces haptic imagery. To enhance efficiency of product touch-ability, researchers propose to arouse the consumer sense of touch even when she/he is shopping online. Indeed, online shopper is not in capacity to touch product presented on the device, but she/he is not deprived of her/his sense of touch and still characterised by a need for touch (Peck and Childers 2003). During online shopping, consumers' tactile sensory captors are stimulated by her/his direct physical environment and this stimulation interact with online experience. On the one hand, tactile stimulation coming from physical environment may be induced by a direct contact of fingers with the device. In this case, "tactile devices" such as tablets induce a higher feeling of ownership towards the product presented on the screen than a simple mouse does (Brasel and Gips 2014, 2015). On the other hand, tactile stimulation coming from physical environment may be induced by any tangible piece of the real consumers' environment such as her/his clothes. When touching a piece of clothes before been exposed to a touch-able product—a product with an enhanced visual texture—online shoppers tend to evaluate this product more favourably than a non-touch-able one (Ferreira et al. 2013). In other words, during online shopping experience, even if the shopper can't touch the product, her/his sense of touch is stimulated by her/his real environment and this tactile stimulation impacts the evaluation of the product presented on the screen by a transfer effect. This tactile sensation transfer effect is enhanced when product presented on the screen has been designed for reaching a high touch-ability level.

References

Alba, J., C. Janiszewski, R. Lutz, A. Sawyer, and S. Wood. 1997a. "Achat Interactif à Domicile: Quels Avantages Pour Les Consommateurs, Les Distributeurs et Les Producteurs Présents Sur Le Marché Électronique." *Journal of Marketing*. https://doi.org/10.1177/076737019801300306.

Alba, Joseph, John Lynch, Barton Weitz, Chris Janiszewski, Richard Lutz, Alan Sawyer, and Stacy Wood. 1997b. "Interactive Home Shopping: Consumer, Retailer, and Manufacturer Incentives to Participate in Electronic Marketplaces." *Journal of Marketing* 61 (3): 38. https://doi.org/10.2307/1251788.

Argo, Jennifer J., Darren W. Dahl, and Andrea C. Morales. 2006. "Consumer Contamination: How Consumers React to Products Touched by Others." *Journal of Marketing* 70 (2l): 81–94.

Bagozzi, R. P. 2007. "The Legacy of the Technology Acceptance Model and a Proposal for a Paradigm Shift." *Journal of the Association for Information Systems* 8 (4): 244–54. http://aisel.aisnet.org/jais/vol8/iss4/3/.

Bagozzi, R. P., and K. H. Lee. 1999. "Consumer Resistance to, and Acceptance of, Innovations." *Advances in Consumer Research* 26: 218–25. http://search.ebscohost.com/login.aspx?direct=true&profile=ehost&scope=site&authtype=crawler&jrnl=00989258&AN=83144281&h=h4uA0ubISVOuPG/BzUANke/S/ndRg5qL4sXAtO/f84mOIZBEDPrskkAM6NfdxlRutFlscNY8Opr0g4BOOQaKHg==&crl=c.

Barsalou, Lawrence W. 2010. "Grounded Cognition: Past, Present, and Future." *Topics in Cognitive Science* 2 (4): 716–24. https://doi.org/10.1111/j.1756-8765.2010.01115.x.

Bèzes, Christophe. 2012. "Une Comparaison Empirique Du Profil Des Acheteurs Monocanal et Multicanaux." *Management & Avenir* 52 (2): 119–37. https://doi.org/10.3917/mav.052.0119.

Biocca, Frank. 1992. "Virtual Reality Technology: A Tutorial." *Journal of Communication* 42 (4): 23–72. https://doi.org/10.1111/j.1460-2466.1992.tb00811.x.

———. 2003. "Can We Resolve the Book, the Physical Reality, and the Dream State Problems? From the Two-Pole to a Three-Pole Model of Shifts in Presence." In *EU Future and Emerging Technologies Presence Initiative Meeting*. http://www.mindlab.org/images/d/DOC705.pdf.

Bouvier, Patrice. 2008. "The Five Pillars of Presence: Guidelines to Reach Presence." In *Proceedings of the 11th Annual International Workshop on Presence*, October, 246–49.

Brasel, S. Adam, and James Gips. 2014. "Tablets, Touchscreens, and Touchpads: How Varying Touch Interfaces Trigger Psychological Ownership and Endowment." *Journal of Consumer Psychology* 24 (2): 226–33. https://doi.org/10.1016/j.jcps.2013.10.003.

———. 2015. "Interface Psychology: Touchscreens Change Attribute Importance, Decision Criteria, and Behavior in Online Choice." *Cyberpsychology, Behavior, and Social Networking* 18 (9): 534–38. https://doi.org/10.1089/cyber.2014.0546.

Bridges, Eileen, and Renée Florsheim. 2008. "Hedonic and Utilitarian Shopping Goals: The Online Experience." *Journal of Business Research* 61 (4): 309–14. https://doi.org/10.1016/j.jbusres.2007.06.017.

Burke, Raymond R. 1997. "Do You See What I See? The Future of Virtual Shopping." *Journal of the Academy of Marketing Science* 4 (25):

352–60. http://scholar.google.com/scholar?hl=en&btnG=Search&q=intitle:Do+you+see+what+I+see#3.

———. 2002. "Technology and the Customer Interface: What Consumers Want in the Physical and Virtual Store." *Journal of the Academy of Marketing Science* 30 (4): 411–32. https://doi.org/10.1177/009207002236914.

———. 2009. "Behavioral Effects of Digital Signage." *Journal of Advertising Research* 49 (2): 180. https://doi.org/10.2501/S0021849909090254.

Chen, Quimei, Sandra J. Clifford, and William D. Wells. 2002. "Attitude Toward the Site II: New Information." *Journal of Advertising Research* 42 (2): 33–45. http://scholar.google.com/scholar?hl=en&btnG=Search&q=intitle:Attitude+Toward+the+Site+II+:+New+information#0.

Chen, Ying-Hueih, I-Chieh Hsu, and Chia-Chen Lin. 2010. "Website Attributes That Increase Consumer Purchase Intention: A Conjoint Analysis." *Journal of Business Research* 63 (9–10): 1007–14. https://doi.org/10.1016/j.jbusres.2009.01.023.

Childers, Terry L., Christopher L. Carr, Joann Peck, and Stephen Carson. 2001. "Hedonic and Utilitarian Motivations for Online Retail Shopping Behavior." *Journal of Retailing* 77 (4): 511–35.

Choi, Yung Kyun, and Charles R. Taylor. 2014. "How Do 3-Dimensional Images Promote Products on the Internet?" *Journal of Business Research* 67 (10): 2164–70. https://doi.org/10.1016/j.jbusres.2014.04.026.

Citrin, Alka Varma, Donald E. Stem, Eric R. Spangenberg, and Michael J. Clark. 2003. "Consumer Need for Tactile Input: An Internet Retailing Challenge." *Journal of Business Research* 56 (11): 915–22. https://doi.org/10.1016/S0148-2963(01)00278-8.

Collin-Lachaud, I., and R. Vanheems. 2016. "Naviguer Entre Espaces Virtuel et Reel Pour Faire Ses Achats: Exploration de Lexperience de Shopping Hybride." *Recherche et Applications En Marketing* 31 (2): 43–61. https://doi.org/10.1177/0767370115617912.

Coyle, J. R., and Esther Thorson. 2001. "The Effects of Progressive Levels of Interactivity and Vividness in Web Marketing Sites." *Journal of Advertising* 30 (3): 65–77.

Csíkszentmihály, M. 1997. "Finding Flow: The Psychology of Engagement with Everyday Life." *Psychology Today*, August: 1–7. https://doi.org/10.5860/CHOICE.35-1828.

Cummins, Shannon, James W. Peltier, John A. Schibrowsky, and Alexander Nill. 2014. "Consumer Behavior in the Online Context." Edited by Angela Hausman. *Journal of Research in Interactive Marketing* 8 (3): 169–202. https://doi.org/10.1108/JRIM-04-2013-0019.

Davis, F. D. 1986. "A Technology Acceptance Model for Empirically Testing New End-User Information Systems: Theory and Results." *Management.* https://doi.org/oclc/56932490.

———. 1989. "Perceived Usefulness, Perceived Ease of Use, and User Acceptance of Information Technology." *MIS Quarterly* 13 (3): 319. https://doi.org/10.2307/249008.

Davis, Fred D., Richard P. Bagozzi, and Paul R. Warshaw. 1989. "User Acceptance of Computer Technology: A Comparison of Two Theoretical Models." *Management Science* 35 (8): 982–1003. https://doi.org/10.1287/mnsc.35.8.982.

———. 1992. "Extrinsic and Intrinsic Motivation to Use Computers in the Workplace1." *Journal of Applied Social Psychology* 22 (14): 1111–32. https://doi.org/10.1111/j.1559-1816.1992.tb00945.x.

Dholakia, Ruby Roy, Miao Zhao, and Nikhilesh Dholakia. 2005. "Multichannel Retailing: A Case Study of Early Experiences." *Journal of Interactive Marketing* 19 (2): 64–74. https://doi.org/10.1002/dir.20035.

Dishaw, Mark T., and Diane M. Strong. 1999. "Extending the Technology Acceptance Model with Task–Technology Fit Constructs." *Information & Management* 36 (1): 9–21. https://doi.org/10.1016/S0378-7206(98)00101-3.

Eklund, Andreas Aldogan, and Miralem Helmefalk. 2018. "Seeing Through Touch: A Conceptual Framework of Visual-Tactile Interplay." *Journal of Product and Brand Management* 27 (5): 498–513. https://doi.org/10.1108/JPBM-07-2017-1520.

Ellis, S. R. 1991. "Nature and Origins of Virtual Environments: A Bibliographical Essay." *Computing Systems in Engineering* 2 (4): 321–47. http://www.sciencedirect.com/science/article/pii/095605219190001L.

Etzi, R., and Gallace, A. 2016. "The Arousing Power of Everyday Materials: An Analysis of the Physiological and Behavioral Responses to Visually and Tactually Presented Textures." *Experimental Brain Research* 234 (6): 1659–66.

Ferreira, Bruno, Sonia Capelli, and Olivier Trendel. 2013. "Le Rôle de La Texture Du Packaging Lors d'un Achat En Ligne." In *29ème Congrès de l'Association Française Du Marketing*, 15–16. La Rochelle.

Flavián, Carlos, Sergio Ibáñez-Sánchez, and Carlos Orús. 2019. "The Impact of Virtual, Augmented and Mixed Reality Technologies on the Customer Experience." *Journal of Business Research* 100 (October): 547–60. https://doi.org/10.1016/j.jbusres.2018.10.050.

Fox, Jesse, Dylan Arena, and Jeremy N. Bailenson. 2009. "Virtual Reality: A Survival Guide for the Social Scientist." *Journal of Media Psychology* 21 (3): 95–113. https://doi.org/10.1027/1864-1105.21.3.95.

Fuchs, Philippe, and Guillaume Moreau. 2006. *Le Traité de La Réalité Virtuelle - Création Des Environnements Virtuels & Applications*. Edited by Philippe Fuchs and Guillaume Moreau. Paris: Presse de.

Gefen, D., Elena Karahanna, and D. W. Straub. 2003. "Trust and TAM in Online Shopping: An Integrated Model." *MIS Quarterly* 27 (1): 51–90.

Gibson, J. J. 1978. "The Ecological Approach to the Visual Perception of Pictures." *Leonardo* 11 (3): 227–35.

Grewal, Dhruv, Gopalkrishnan R. Iyer, and Michael Levy. 2004. "Internet Retailing: Enablers, Limiters and Market Consequences." *Journal of Business Research* 57 (7): 703–13. https://doi.org/10.1016/S0148-2963(02)00348-X.

Grewal, Dhruv, Anne L. Roggeveen, and Jens Nordfält. 2017. "The Future of Retailing." *Journal of Retailing* 93 (1): 1–6. https://doi.org/10.1016/j.jretai.2016.12.008.

Grohmann, Bianca, Eric R. Spangenberg, and David E. Sprott. 2007. "The Influence of Tactile Input on the Evaluation of Retail Product Offerings." *Journal of Retailing* 83 (2): 237–45. https://doi.org/10.1016/j.jretai.2006.09.001.

Grundwald, Martin. 2008. *Human Haptic Perception, Basic and Applications*. Edited by Martin Grundwald. Berlin: Birkhäuser.

Ha, Sejin, and Leslie Stoel. 2009. "Consumer E-Shopping Acceptance: Antecedents in a Technology Acceptance Model." *Journal of Business Research* 62 (5): 565–71.

Hand, Chris. 1997. "A Survey of 3D Interaction Techniques." *Computer Graphics Forum* 16 (5): 269–81.

Hauswiesner, Stefan, Matthias Straka, and Gerhard Reitmayr. 2013. "Virtual Try-on Through Image-Based Rendering." *IEEE Transactions on Visualization and Computer Graphics* 19 (9): 1552–65. https://doi.org/10.1109/TVCG.2013.67.

Heijden, Hans Van Der, Tibert Verhagen, and Marcel Creemers. 2003. "Understanding Online Purchase Intentions: Contributions from Technology and Trust Perspectives." *European Journal of Information Systems* 12 (1): 41–48. https://doi.org/10.1057/palgrave.ejis.3000445.

Hennig-Thurau, Thorsten, Charles F. Hofacker, and Björn Bloching. 2013. "Marketing the Pinball Way: Understanding How Social Media Change the Generation of Value for Consumers and Companies." *Journal of Interactive Marketing* 27 (4): 237–41. https://doi.org/10.1016/j.intmar.2013.09.005.

Hofacker, Charles F. 2012. "On Research Methods in Interactive Marketing." *Journal of Interactive Marketing* 26 (1): 1–3. https://doi.org/10.1016/j.intmar.2011.10.001.

Hoffman, Donna L., and Thomas P. Novak. 1996. "Marketing in Hypermedia Computer-Mediated Environments: Conceptual Foundations." *Journal of Marketing* 60 (3): 50. https://doi.org/10.2307/1251841.

———. 2009. "Flow Online: Lessons Learned and Future Prospects." *Journal of Interactive Marketing* 23 (1): 23–34. https://doi.org/10.1016/j.intmar.2008.10.003.

Hoffman, Donna L., Thomas P. Novak, and Alladi Venkatesh. 2004. "Has the Internet Become Indispensable?" *Communications of the ACM* 47 (7): 37–42. https://doi.org/10.1145/1005817.1005818.

Hsu, Chia-Lin, Kuo-Chien Chang, and Mu-Chen Chen. 2012. "The Impact of Website Quality on Customer Satisfaction and Purchase Intention: Perceived Playfulness and Perceived Flow as Mediators." *Information Systems and E-Business Management* 10 (4): 549–70. https://doi.org/10.1007/s10257-011-0181-5.

Hung, Kineta H., and Stella Yiyan Li. 2007. "The Influence of EWOM on Virtual Consumer Communities: Social Capital, Consumer Learning, and Behavioral Outcomes." *Journal of Advertising Research* 47 (4): 485. https://doi.org/10.2501/S002184990707050X.

Jiang, Zhenhui, and Izak Benbasat. 2004. "Virtual Product Experience: Effects of Visual and Functional Control of Products on Perceived Diagnosticity and Flow in Electronic Shopping." *Journal of Management Information Systems* 21 (3): 111–47. https://doi.org/10.1080/07421222.2004.11045817.

———. 2007. "The Effects of Presentation Formats and Task Complexity on Online Consumers' Product Understanding." *MIS Quarterly* 31 (3): 475. https://doi.org/10.2307/25148804.

Kannan, P. K., and Hongshuang "Alice" Li. 2017. "Digital Marketing: A Framework, Review and Research Agenda." *International Journal of Research in Marketing* 34 (1): 22–45. https://doi.org/10.1016/j.ijresmar.2016.11.006.

Kaplan, A. M., and M. Haenlein. 2009. "Utilisation et Potentiel Commercial Des Hyperréalités: Une Analyse Qualitative de Second Life." *Revue Française Du Marketing* 222 (2–5): 69–81. http://dialnet.unirioja.es/servlet/articulo?codigo=3009335.

Kardong-Edgren, Suzan (Suzie), Sharon L. Farra, Guillaume Alinier, and H. Michael Young. 2019. "A Call to Unify Definitions of Virtual Reality." *Clinical Simulation in Nursing* 31 (June): 28–34. https://doi.org/10.1016/j.ecns.2019.02.006.

Katz, James, and Philip Aspden. 1997. "Motives, Hurdles, and Dropouts." *Communications of the ACM* 40 (4): 97–102. https://doi.org/10.1145/248448.248464.

Keen, Cherie, Martin Wetzels, Ko de Ruyter, and Richard Feinberg. 2004. "E-Tailers Versus Retailers." *Journal of Business Research* 57 (7): 685–95.

Kerrebroeck, Helena Van, Kim Willems, and Malaika Brengman. 2017. "Touching the Void: Exploring Consumer Perspectives on Touch-Enabling Technologies in Online Retailing." *International Journal of Retail and Distribution Management* 45 (7–8): 892–909. https://doi.org/10.1108/IJRDM-09-2016-0156.

Kim, Jiyeon, and Sandra Forsythe. 2008a. "Adoption of Virtual Try-on Technology for Online Apparel Shopping." *Journal of Interactive Marketing* 22 (2): 45–59. https://doi.org/10.1002/dir.20113.

———. 2008b. "Sensory Enabling Technology Acceptance Model (SE-TAM): A Multiple-Group Structural Model Comparison." *Psychology and Marketing* 25 (9): 901–22. https://doi.org/10.1002/mar.20245.

Klatzky, Roberta L., and Joann Peck. 2012. "Please Touch: Object Properties That Invite Touch." *IEEE Transactions on Haptics* 5 (2): 139–47. https://doi.org/10.1109/TOH.2011.54.

Kock, Ned. 2004. "The Psychobiological Model: Towards a New Theory of Computer-Mediated Communication Based on Darwinian Evolution." *Organization Science* 15 (3): 327–48. https://doi.org/10.1287/orsc.1040.0071.

———. 2005. "Media Richness or Media Naturalness? The Evolution of Our Biological Communication Apparatus and Its Influence on Our Behavior Toward e-Communication Tools." *IEEE Transactions on Professional Communication* 48 (2): 117–30. https://doi.org/10.1109/TPC.2005.849649.

Krishna, Aradhna. 2012. "An Integrative Review of Sensory Marketing: Engaging the Senses to Affect Perception, Judgment and Behavior." *Journal of Consumer Psychology* 22 (3): 332–51. https://doi.org/10.1016/j.jcps.2011.08.003.

Krishna, Aradhna, and Norbert Schwarz. 2014. "Sensory Marketing, Embodiment, and Grounded Cognition: A Review and Introduction." *Journal of Consumer Psychology* 24 (2): 159–68. https://doi.org/10.1016/j.jcps.2013.12.006.

Lee, K. M. 2004. "Presence, Explicated." *Communication Theory* 14 (1): 27–50. https://doi.org/10.1093/ct/14.1.27.

Li, Hairong, Terry Daugherty, and Frank Biocca. 2001. "Characteristics of Virtual Experience in Electronic Commerce: A Protocol Analysis." *Journal of Interactive Marketing* 15 (3): 13. https://doi.org/10.1002/dir.1013.

———. 2002. "Impact of 3-D Advertising on Product Knowledge, Brand Attitude, and Purchase Intention: The Mediating Role of Presence." *Journal of Advertising* XXXI (3): 43–57. https://doi.org/10.1080/00913367.2002.10673675.

———. 2003. "The Role of Virtual Experience in Consumer Learning." *Journal of Consumer Psychology* 13 (4): 395–407. https://doi.org/10.1207/S15327663JCP1304_07.

Lombard, M., and Ditton, T. B. 2001. "Measuring Presence: A Literature-Based Approach to the Development of a Standardized Paper and Pencil Instrument." Paper presented at Presence 2001: The Third International Workshop on Presence, Philadelphia.

Martínez-Navarro, Jesus, Enrique Bigné, Jaime Guixeres, Mariano Alcañiz, and Carmen Torrecilla. 2019. "The Influence of Virtual Reality in E-Commerce." *Journal of Business Research* 100 (October): 475–82. https://doi.org/10.1016/j.jbusres.2018.10.054.

McCole, Patrick, Elaine Ramsey, and John Williams. 2010. "Trust Considerations on Attitudes Towards Online Purchasing: The Moderating Effect of Privacy and Security Concerns." *Journal of Business Research* 63 (9–10): 1018–24. https://doi.org/10.1016/j.jbusres.2009.02.025.

McLean, Graeme, and Kofi Osei-Frimpong. 2019. "Hey Alexa … Examine the Variables Influencing the Use of Artificial Intelligent In-Home Voice Assistants." *Computers in Human Behavior* 99 (May): 28–37. https://doi.org/10.1016/j.chb.2019.05.009.

McLellan, H. 1996. "Virtual Realities." In *Handbook of Research for Educational Communications and Technology*, edited by D. H. Jonassen, 457–87. New York: Macmillan.

Meng, Yuwei, P. Y. Mok, and Xiaogang Jin. 2010. "Interactive Virtual Try-on Clothing Design Systems." *CAD Computer Aided Design* 42 (4): 310–21. https://doi.org/10.1016/j.cad.2009.12.004.

Merle, Aurélie, Sylvain Sénécal, and Anik St-Onge. 2012. "Whether and How Virtual Try-on Influences Consumer Responses to an Apparel Web Site." *International Journal of Electronic Commerce* 16 (3): 41–64. https://doi.org/10.2753/JEC1086-4415160302.

Micu, Anca Cristina, Kim Dedeker, Ian Lewis, Robert Moran, Oded Netzer, Joseph Plummer, and Joel Rubinson. 2011. "The Shape of Marketing Research in 2021." *Journal of Advertising Research* 51 (1): 213–21. https://doi.org/10.2501/JAR-51-1-213-221.

Milgram, Paul, Haruo Takemura, Akira Utsumi, and Fumio Kishino. 1994. "Augmented Reality: A Class of Displays on the Reality-Virtuality Continuum." In *Telemanipulator and Telepresence Technologies*, edited by Hari Das, 2351, 282–92. https://doi.org/10.1117/12.197321.

Minsky, M. 1980. "Telepresence." *Omni* 2: 45–51.

Noort, Guda van, Hilde A. M. Voorveld, and Eva A. van Reijmersdal. 2012. "Interactivity in Brand Web Sites: Cognitive, Affective, and Behavioral Responses Explained by Consumers' Online Flow Experience." *Journal of Interactive Marketing* 26 (4): 223–34. https://doi.org/10.1016/j.intmar.2011.11.002.

Overmars, Suzanne, and Karolien Poels. 2015. "Online Product Experiences: The Effect of Simulating Stroking Gestures on Product Understanding and the Critical Role of User Control." *Computers in Human Behavior* 51 (PA): 272–84. https://doi.org/10.1016/j.chb.2015.04.033.

Pagani, Margherita, Margot Racat, and Charles F. Hofacker. 2019. "Adding Voice to the Omnichannel and How That Affects Brand Trust." *Journal of Interactive Marketing* 48: 89–105. https://doi.org/10.1016/j.intmar.2019.05.002.

Parisi, David. 2008. "Fingerbombing or 'Touching Is Good': The Cultural Construction of Technologized Touch." *Senses & Society* 3 (3): 307–27.

———. 2014. "Reach In and Feel Something: On the Strategic Reconstruction of Touch in Virtual Space." *Animation: An Interdisciplinary Journal* 9 (2): 228–44. https://doi.org/10.1177/1746847714527195.

———. 2018. *Archaeologies of Touch: Interfacing with Haptics from Electricity to Computing*. Minneapolis: University of Minnesota Press.

Parisi, David, Mark Paterson, and Jason Edward Archer. 2017. "Haptic Media Studies." *New Media and Society*, October 3. https://doi.org/10.1177/1461444817717518.

Peck, Joann, and T. L. Childers. 2003. "Individual Differences in Haptic Information Processing: The 'Need for Touch' Scale." *Journal of Consumer Research* 30 (3): 430–43.

Peck, Joann, Victor A. Barger, and Andrea Webb. 2013. "In Search of a Surrogate for Touch: The Effect of Haptic Imagery on Perceived Ownership." *Journal of Consumer Psychology* 23 (2): 189–96.

Poncin, Ingrid, and Marion Garnier. 2010. "L'expérience Sur Un Site de Vente 3D. Le Vrai, Le Faux et Le Virtuel: À La Croisée Des Chemins." *Management & Avenir* 32 (2): 173–91. http://www.cairn.info/revue-management-et-avenir-2010-2-page-173.htm.

Racat, Margot, and Sonia Capelli. 2014. "Le Test Virtuel Des Produits Influence-t-Il La Décision d'achat En Ligne?" *Revue Française Du Marketing* 250: 27–39. https://www.scopus.com/inward/record.uri?eid=2-s2.0-84968586447&partnerID=40&md5=6c2409bbfe17ea4fac53e817e4345b1c.

———. 2016. "L'impact de La Similarité Sur l'efficacité Des Outils d'aide à La Vente En Ligne." *Revue Francaise de Gestion* 254 (1): 89–105. https://doi.org/10.3166/rfg.2016.00005.

Reeves, B. 1991. "'Being There': Television as Symbolic Versus Natural Experience." Unpublished Manuscript, Institute for Communication Research, Stanford University, Stanford, CA.

Rheingold, H. 1991. *Virtual Reality.* New York: Summit Books.

Rinaldo, Shannon Bridgmon. 2008. "The Interaction of Haptic Imagery with Haptic Perception for Sighted and Visually Impaired Consumers." University of Kentucky. http://uknowledge.uky.edu/gradschool_diss/687/.

Roggeveen, Anne L., Dhruv Grewal, Claudia Townsend, and R. Krishnan. 2015. "The Impact of Dynamic Presentation Format on Consumer Preferences for Hedonic Products and Services." *Journal of Marketing* 79 (November): 1–16. https://doi.org/10.1509/jm.13.0521.

Rozin, Paul, Linda Millman, and Carol Nemeroff. 1986. "Operation of the Laws of Sympathetic Magic in Disgust and Other Domains." *Journal of Personality and Social Psychology* 50 (4): 703–12. https://doi.org/10.1037/0022-3514.50.4.703.

Schepers, Jeroen, and Martin Wetzels. 2007. "A Meta-Analysis of the Technology Acceptance Model: Investigating Subjective Norm and Moderation Effects." *Information & Management* 44 (1): 90–103. https://doi.org/10.1016/j.im.2006.10.007.

Schloerb, D. W. 1995. "A Quantitative Measure of Telepresence." *Presence: Teleoperators and Virtual Environments* 4: 64–80.

Schlosser, A. E. 2003. "Experiencing Products in the Virtual World: The Role of Goal and Imagery in Influencing Attitudes versus Purchase Intentions." *Journal of Consumer Research* 30 (2): 184–99.

———. 2006. "Learning Through Virtual Product Experience: The Role of Imagery on True Versus False Memories." *Journal of Consumer Research* 33 (3): 377–83. https://doi.org/10.1086/508522.

Schlosser, Ann E., Tiffany Barnett White, and Susan M. Lloyd. 2006. "Converting Web Site Visitors into Buyers: How Web Site Investment Increases Consumer Trusting Beliefs and Online Purchase Intentions." *Journal of Marketing* 70 (2): 133–48. https://doi.org/10.1509/jmkg.70.2.133.

Shankar, Venkatesh, Alladi Venkatesh, Charles Hofacker, and Prasad Naik. 2010. "Mobile Marketing in the Retailing Environment: Current Insights and Future Research Avenues." *Journal of Interactive Marketing* 24 (2): 111–20. https://doi.org/10.1016/j.intmar.2010.02.006.

Sheridan, Thomas B. 1992. "Musings on Telepresence and Virtual Presence." *Presence: Teleoperators and Virtual Environments* 1 (1): 120–26. https://doi.org/10.1162/pres.1992.1.1.120.

Slater, M., and Usoh, M. 1993. "Representations Systems, Perceptual Position, and Presence in Immersive Virtual Environments." *Presence: Teleoperators and Virtual Environments* 2: 221–33.

Slater, M., and Usoh, M. 1994. "Body Centred Interaction in Immersive Virtual Environments." *Artificial Life and Virtual Reality* 1 (1994): 125–48.

Slater, Mel, and Sylvia Wilbur. 1997. "A Framework for Immersive Virtual Environments (FIVE): Speculations on the Role of Presence in Virtual Environments." *Presence: Teleoperators and Virtual Environments* 6 (6): 603–16. https://doi.org/10.1007/s10750-008-9541-7.

Sreelakshmi, M., and T. D. Subash. 2017. "Haptic Technology: A Comprehensive Review on Its Applications and Future Prospects." *Materials Today: Proceedings* 4 (2): 4182–87. https://doi.org/10.1016/j.matpr.2017.02.120.

Sternberger, M. Ludovic. 2006. "Interaction En Réalité Virtuelle." Université Louis Pasteur de Strasbourg 1.

Steuer, Jonathan. 1992. "Defining Virtual Reality: Dimensions Determining Telepresence." *Journal of Communication* 42 (4): 73–93. https://doi.org/10.1111/j.1460-2466.1992.tb00812.x.

Sutherland, Ivan E. 1965. "The Ultimate Display." *Proceedings of the Congress of the Internation Federation of Information Processing (IFIP)*, 506–8. https://doi.org/10.1109/MC.2005.274.

Varadarajan, Rajan, Raji Srinivasan, Gautham Gopal Vadakkepatt, Manjit S. Yadav, Paul A. Pavlou, Sandeep Krishnamurthy, and Tom Krause. 2010. "Interactive Technologies and Retailing Strategy: A Review, Conceptual Framework and Future Research Directions." *Journal of Interactive Marketing* 24 (2): 96–110. https://doi.org/10.1016/j.intmar.2010.02.004.

Venkatesh, Viswanath, James Y. L. Thong, and Xin Xu. 2012. "Consumer Acceptance and Use of Information Technology: Extending the Unified Theory." *MIS Quarterly* 36 (1): 157–78. https://doi.org/10.1017/CBO9781107415324.004.

Verhoef, Peter C., Andrew T. Stephen, P. K. Kannan, Xueming Luo, Vibhanshu Abhishek, Michelle Andrews, Yakov Bart, H. Datta, N. Fong, D. L. Hoffman, M. M. Hu. 2017. "Consumer Connectivity in a Complex, Technology-Enabled, and Mobile-Oriented World with Smart Products." *Journal of Interactive Marketing* 40: 1–8. https://doi.org/10.1016/j.intmar.2017.06.001.

Vijayasarathy, Leo R. 2004. "Predicting Consumer Intentions to Use On-Line Shopping: The Case for an Augmented Technology Acceptance Model." *Information & Management* 41 (6): 747–62. https://doi.org/10.1016/j.im.2003.08.011.

Wacker, Markus, and Michael Keckeisen. 2005. "Simulation and Visualisation of Virtual Textiles for Virtual Try-on." *Special Issue of Research Journal of Textile and Apparel: Virtual Clothing Technology and Applications* 9 (1): 37–47.

Watson, George F., Stefan Worm, Robert W. Palmatier, and Shankar Ganesan. 2015. "The Evolution of Marketing Channels: Trends and Research Directions." *Journal of Retailing* 91 (4): 546–68. https://doi.org/10.1016/j.jretai.2015.04.002.

Witmer, B. G., and Singer, M. J. 1998. "Measuring Presence in Virtual Environments: A Presence Questionnaire." *Presence* 7 (3): 225–40. https://doi.org/10.1162/105474698565686.

Xiao, Bei, Wenyan Bi, Xiaodan Jia, Hanhan Wei, and Edward H. Adelson. 2016. "Can You See What You Feel? Color and Folding Properties Affect Visual–Tactile Material Discrimination of Fabrics." *Journal of Vision* 16 (3): 34. https://doi.org/10.1167/16.3.34.

Yadav, Manjit S., and Paul A. Pavlou. 2014. "Marketing in Computer-Mediated Environments: Research Synthesis and New Directions." *Journal of Marketing* 78 (1): 20–40. https://doi.org/10.1509/jm.12.0020.

Yadav, Manjit S., Kristine de Valck, Thorsten Hennig-Thurau, Donna L. Hoffman, and Martin Spann. 2013. "Social Commerce: A Contingency Framework for Assessing Marketing Potential." *Journal of Interactive Marketing* 27 (4): 311–23. https://doi.org/10.1016/j.intmar.2013.09.001.

Yang, Shuai, and Guiyang Xiong. 2019. "Try It on! Contingency Effects of Virtual Fitting Rooms." *Journal of Management Information Systems* 36 (3): 789–822. https://doi.org/10.1080/07421222.2019.1628894.

Yim, Mark Yi Cheon, and Sun Young Park. 2019. "'I Am Not Satisfied with My Body, So I like Augmented Reality (AR)': Consumer Responses to AR-Based Product Presentations." *Journal of Business Research* 100 (October): 581–89. https://doi.org/10.1016/j.jbusres.2018.10.041.

Yoshida. 1968. "Dimensions of Tactual Impressions." *Japenese Psychological Research* 10 (3): 123–37.

Zahorik, P., and Jenison, R. L. 1998. "Presence as Being-in-the-World." *Presence* 7 (1): 78–89.

Zwaan, Rolf A. 1999. "Embodied Cognition, Perceptual Symbols, and Situation Models." *Discourse Processes* 28 (1): 81–88. https://doi.org/10.1080/01638539909545070.

3

When Interfaces Make It Real

Abstract This chapter aims to reflect on the role of intermediaries that are interfaces and how their tactile attributes are "integrated" into the processing of information by consumers when browsing and searching for products through the device. We first define and explain the different type of tactile interfaces currently available on the market. Second, we discuss the tactile rendering techniques and benefits from a consumer's perspective for online shopping.

Keywords Realism · Haptic · Force feedback · Tactile rendering · Interaction

This chapter aims to reflect on the role of intermediaries that are interfaces and how their tactile attributes are "integrated" into the processing of information by consumers when browsing and searching for products through the device. We first define and explain the different type of tactile interfaces currently available on the market. Second, we discuss the tactile rendering techniques and benefits from a consumer's perspective for online shopping.

3.1 From Product Touch to the Interface Touch

For the past two decades, Internet development has brought to light the question of how to stimulate and use the sense of touch in virtual consumption (Citrin et al. 2003; Childers et al. 2001; Verhoef et al. 2017; Debrégeas et al. 2009; Yadav and Pavlou 2014). In line with it, Parisi (2018) explains that cultural-based consideration of the visual sense for constructing interfaces has reached a point of saturation of "non-using" our tactile sensitivity, meaning that tactile perception needs to recover its full capacity and role within online environment. Indeed, interfaces allow so far the visual sense to be dominant and widely adapted by reproducing colours, geometrical perspectives (3D, zooming), etc. as introduced in the previous chapter. Yet, as Gleckman (2000) says, "*the lesson here is simple: I always want to see and touch a product before purchase. Internet websites are good for books and plane tickets. But they don't make you feel anything*" (reported in Spence and Gallace 2011).

Chapter 1 reviewed literature of the positive influence of tactile contact on consumers' judgement and purchase decision-making, in particular for tangible products' apprehension (McCabe and Nowlis 2003), while visual exploration lacks tangibility and does not allow for further trust and confidence into the product visualised on the screen (Peck and Childers 2003b; Childers et al. 2001). Consequently, computer-mediation brought more physical distant to products manipulations (Citrin et al. 2003). Yet, interface mediation in online experience does not mean that consumers' sense of touch is not stimulated by the environment: consumers interact with a keyboard, a screen, a mouse, etc. which all provide haptic information that influences product perception and choice (Brasel and Gips 2014, 2015).

3.1.1 Interface Haptic Stimulation and Influence on Consumers' Behaviour

Tactile sensory cues of interfaces recently became of interest for marketers and academic research despite concerns and questions raised for almost two decades (Hoffman and Novak 1996; Varadarajan et al. 2010; Yadav and Pavlou 2014). Nonetheless, research on haptic influence in marketing literature remains scarce while it has been shown that interfaces haptic stimulation influence consumers' online experience as much as for physical consumption (Brasel and Gips 2014, 2015; Shen et al. 2016; Chung et al. 2018; Zhu and Meyer 2017; Blazquez Cano et al. 2017; Racat and Capelli 2016).

Among the first studies on the topic, Brasel and Gips (2014) demonstrated that consumers experience similar ownership feeling towards the product when the interface stimulates directly the sense of touch (i.e. touchscreens). With an experimental plan, they compared different interfaces available for navigating online and showed that tactile interfaces as tablet induce higher ownership feeling than a mouse or pad. As shown in Chapter 2, these three types of interfaces, which enable consumers to interact with products in virtual environment, differ slightly on how consumers use them: for pad and mouse, consumers control the device and tactile interactions occur through it while, for the tactile interfaces, consumers' tactile interaction is more direct with the visual online representation of the product. As a result, Brasel and Gips (2014) confirm that the tactile interface brings more direct experience of the product than the mouse and pad, inducing that the tablet is more seamless to consumers in online interactions (Daugherty et al. 2008). Further research extends these findings and shows that these different interfaces influence consumers' purchase intention by modifying consumers' thinking style such as the more the interface is tactile-based (i.e. control occurs directly on the screen with the product image), the more consumers set their mind in experiential configuration compared to the computer that induces more rational thinking style (Zhu and Meyer 2017). Particularly, the experiential thinking style, prompted by touchscreens, endorses more hedonic products while rational thinking style, prompted by more distant interfaces, endorses more utilitarian products. Moreover, touchscreens engage more consumers into their online shopping experience, particularly with higher image interactivity and for consumers showing lower involvement (i.e. browsing) (Chung et al. 2018; Blazquez Cano et al. 2017). In sum, touchscreens lead to more hedonic consumption which further confirms previous results by Shen et al. (2016) who showed that the "direct touch" effect of the tactile interfaces influence consumers' preference for hedonic products. Therefore, the tactile cues of interfaces allowing to interact virtually with products influence consumers' perception and behavioural responses.

Yet, further sensory modalities now extend the tactile and visual cues of interface by adding voice interaction. Indeed, recent innovations imply that, when interacting with touchscreen devices such as smartphones, consumers can use alternative methods to interact with and access virtual environments. On the one hand, beyond visual apprehension, consumers use touch to search, select and interact with product information and brands while, on the other hand, when they add vocal command in their interaction, consumers use both passive and active forms of touch—i.e. when "talking" to the smartphone, consumers hold the device inducing haptic stimulation. Thus, when considering this dual interaction, recent findings show that touching the interface increase more consumers' engagement and trust towards brands than voice and tactile interaction together, for both product type—i.e. hedonic or utilitarian (Pagani et al. 2019). Yet, the authors remain cautious on their results since further studies on multisensory interactions through the device are needed to develop consumers' understanding on how the device is interpreted, beside familiarity with new sensory integration. In other terms, according to Kock (2004, 2005), it is expected that vocal interaction increases furthermore the natural communication mode despite the interface mediation. Unfortunately, with the successful introduction of Alexa, Google Home or Hound devices, that gives priority to vocal interaction, interfaces sensory cues reduce again the tactile interaction within the virtual environments while it is a necessary input for consumers as previous research shows. For this reason, we question at this stage the real integration of various sensory modalities through the interface for creating a fluid and natural interaction allowing to perceived products and create bonds without cutting each sense in the process. In this sense, research on the tactile role of interfaces needs further implementation, and, particularly, to explore how the addition of other senses in the mediated interaction influences the tactile perception of online products.

3.1.2 Consumers' Evolution of Touching in Computer-Mediated Environments

Touching through interfaces consists of interacting with virtual objects, people or product that remains grounded into other physical dimensions. According to the grounded cognition theory (Barsalou 2008), the senses do not differentiate between two environments: hands, as an organ, allow for haptic exploration and receive direct tactile input from the environment, but this is the mental abstract treatment that leads to a behaviour. Consequently, hands do not differentiate the direct tactile input of an interface (direct environment) from an indirect product manipulation (mediated by an interface): this is the human mental representation at abstract level that provides the ability to formulate a difference and understand the difference between direct and indirect environments (Daugherty et al. 2008; Barsalou 1999). In other words, by adding the missing product haptic interaction, the virtual interaction is no longer another and far dimension of the consumer's experience but rather the actual physical reality of the consumption environments, meaning that the interface becomes "transparent" to the consumer (Barsalou 2003; Vermeulen et al. 2008; Steuer 1992; Fuchs and Moreau 2006).

However, considering perceptual information processing, touching virtual product differs from touching actual product: tactile receptors receive a physical input that prompt consumers' behaviour that is unrelated to the targeted content. Thus, investigating computer-mediated touch means to search for psychophysiological transfer but also for new types of interaction generated by the global consumption environment that includes interfaces as full part of the perceptual information processing (Flavián et al. 2019; Racat 2016). For instance, when investigating social touch, research on psychological transfer of the Midas touch in virtual environments remains cautious on finding similar effects than in physical settings (Haans et al. 2014). Indeed, through a series of experiments, their results indicate limited support for it, which confirms the potential non-transferrable tactile effect or, at least, in different manner not yet identified. From another perspective, research on consumers product interaction shows that use of similar haptic gestures in online environments enable consumers to better feel control and vivid interaction that further increase product understanding as if it was in physical conditions (Overmars and Poels 2015; Schlosser 2006; Jiang and Benbasat 2004), although these touchscreen interactions remain far from the actual physical contact with products (Daugherty et al. 2008; Racat 2016).

In 2019, the number of interfaces surrounding consumers makes it difficult to avoid for daily social and consumption interactions. Hence, the market now distinguishes tactile interactions between wearables (i.e. smart watches)—often related to Internet of Things, touch screens (i.e. smartphones, tablets), and non-tactile devices (i.e. computers) (Dangxiao et al. 2019). Further classification also considers the embodiment of interfaces as main factor—i.e. technology is more and more integrated in and extending the human body (Flavián et al. 2019). As a result, each device induces new types of tactile sensations from the biological human perspective (Kock 2004). For instance, people born before 1980 did not have such interfaces to grow with compared to the new generations who have deeply integrated interfaces as a regular interactive medium (Hardey 2011). In that, apprehension of "non-natural" sensory load differs from previous generations such as youngers do not consider technologies as a barrier to experience products and services as elder generations do (Giebelhausen et al. 2014). Indeed, when observing children born after 2000, they seem to experience easier and seamlessly social interactions and online consumption environments through interfaces (Joiner et al. 2013). Especially, their behaviours demonstrate a natural tendency for using online tools and interfaces such as tablets and smartphones without questioning the absence or different tactile interactions. Furthermore, they show finer and more accurate apprehension of tactile interaction with the device whereas they never actually learnt to "swipe", "double tape", etc. in real-life organisation to obtain a reaction from the product or another person. However, related literature is limited and concentrates more on actual influence of tactile devices on online trust or addiction behaviour for instance (Mulcahy and Riedel 2018; Hoffmann et al. 2014), instead of investigating the impact of merging environments such as the before dissociated environments become now one and only (Biocca 1992; Parisi 2014; Racat 2016; Racat and Capelli 2016; Steuer

1992). Yet, to obtain seamlessly experience between physical and online consumption environments, haptic rendering techniques and technologies still need further improvement although current implementation successfully stimulates consumers' tactile sense.

3.2 Tactile Rendering Systems: Recovering Haptic Experiences

The human haptic system relies on stimulation of tactile receptors that arises from mechanical signals such as forces, contact, torques, movements of objects and limbs, mass or weight of objects, stiffness of materials or their geometry. In virtual environments, haptic stimulation relies on the sensory signals sent by the interface, which are designated as haptic interfaces (Robles-De-La-Torre 2008).

Parisi (2018) situates around the eighteenth century the emergence of tactile media (pp. 95–97). According to him, contemporary touch-based interfaces, commonly called Haptic Interfaces, rose by this time with a reverse research objective that was first to understand electricity itself. By then, touch was considered as the mean to obtain this knowledge but never as a research object itself. By the nineteenth century, the contrary occurred slowly by moving from being the media to understand electricity to being, through electrical experiments, the tactile mechanism to understand. As such, touch and tactile processes became the centre of experiences with protocols based on electricity. Moreover, and beyond the changing focus, Parisi (2018) underlines the important shift of tactile media functioning such as "*where initially, tactile media depended on the translation of mechanical energy into electricity via the electrostatic generator and then subsequently of electricity into electro tactile shock, today's tactile media frequently depend on the reverse mechanism – transforming electrical energy into motion – to create and render tactual effect*" (p. 97). Hence, the reverse process marks the beginning of new haptic considerations for building tactile rendering interfaces aimed for consumption.

3.2.1 Tactile Rendering Technologies: Functioning and Developments

Since the first attempts of virtual reality by the 1950s with Heilig, research in computer sciences and robotics aims at including the whole range of senses to transcribe the full sensory experience that is known in the physical reality (Sutherland 1965). In this way, haptic rendering is the processing of determining a reaction force for a given position of the haptic device enabling bilateral signal communication as for physical interactions (Laycock and Day 2007). Another definition states that haptic rendering is the process of computing and generating forces in response to user interaction with virtual objects (Salisbury et al. 1995). Unfortunately, developments aimed at mass markets faced, for a long time, economic, cultural and political considerations that lead to launch more accessible and, thus, less complex apparatus (Grundwald 2008; Parisi 2018). Nevertheless, tactile influence has never really been neglected since tactile rendering technologies broke into consumption markets[1] by the end of the 1980s with the first version of today's digital tablets (e.g. iPad, Microsoft Surface, etc.).

Technically, rendering haptic sensations through touchscreens varies from friction, force feedback (i.e. mechanical vibrations) and surface modifications, and these techniques are continuously improved (Laycock and Day 2007; Kim et al. 2013; Allerkamp et al. 2007; Philpott and Summers 2012; Zeng et al. 2010; Camillieri et al. 2018; Dangxiao et al. 2019; Gueorguiev et al. 2017; Unger et al. 2011; Skedung et al. 2011) (Fig. 3.1).

Besides, haptic interfaces rely on two types of haptic structuration stimulating kinaesthetic and proprioceptive perception (Fuchs and Moreau 2003). On the one hand, kinaesthetic interfaces relate to kinaesthesia perception which enables to determine pressure, object volume, density and temperature while, on the other hand, proprioceptive interfaces enable to evaluate movements and forces in contact. The latest also allows for spatial representation. Considering markets and consumption, behavioural interfaces are the type of interfaces that come

---

[1] https://www.futura-sciences.com/tech/dossiers/technologie-tablettes-essor-tactile-1472/page/4/.

Mechanical vibration	ERM - eccentric rotating-mass actuators LRA – linear resonant actuators Piezoelectric actuators Voice coil vibrators
Surface shape modification	Pin array Electrode array Pneumatic chambers
Friction forces	Squeeze-film effect Electrostatic effect

Fig. 3.1 List of current main haptic rendering systems

closer to seamless experiences between physical and virtual environments. Fuchs and Moreau (2003) define this category as an apparatus that uses human sensory and motor perception, which corresponds nowadays to wearable devices, although haptic rendering still needs further improvements to render realistic sensations. The authors particularly state that behavioural interface prevents from consumers' learning stage since the natural approach based on human physical characteristics makes it easier and innate. However, current haptic interfaces (i.e. smartphone, wearables devices, and tablets) generate haptic rendering based on a bilateral communication purposes and model mainly—i.e. vibrations to indicate the impact of an action or to indicate the reception of information from the virtual environment as messages, call, etc. Hence, it is possible to classify haptic interfaces based on their tactile cues (Fig. 3.2) and tactile stimulation effect on consumers (Table 3.1).

Yet rendering capacities concentrates so far on geometrical features detection of virtual objects[2] compared to texture identification. Accordingly, consumers can detect objects in virtual spaces or receive confirmation that their action has been completed, which changes their perception of the virtual environment (Kim et al. 2013). For instance, Jin (2011) demonstrates that consumers with higher instrumental need for touch appreciate more a virtual car test-driving experience, connects more with the brand and evaluate better the product when the haptic rendering device provides tactile feedback when interacting. Nonetheless,

---

[2] https://www.youtube.com/watch?v=zo1n5CyCKr0.

Desktop devices	Touchscreens	Wearables
a, b  	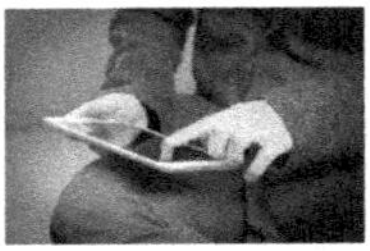 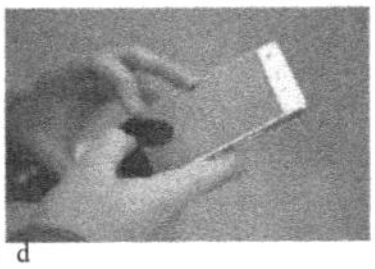 c, d	e 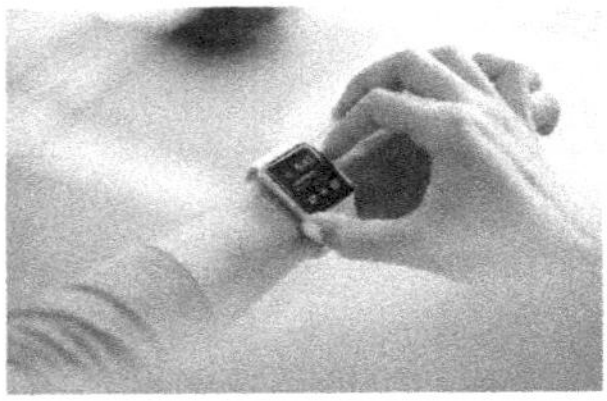
Click or finger tap	Finger pressure and movements (swipe, double tap)	Finger tactile movements (swipe, double tap) and force feedback information with skin.

Fig. 3.2 Tactile classification of devices based on consumers' haptic interaction (*Source* [a]Image parOpenClipart-Vectors de Pixabay—Free of use. [b]Image parhamonazaryan1 de Pixabay—Free of use. [c]Image parNiek Verlaan de Pixabay—Free of use. [d]Image parPexels de Pixabay—Free of use. [e]Image by Free-Photos de Pixabay—Free of use)

haptic systems mostly render spatial and geometrical cues of the virtual information while, surprisingly, the relation between the interface and product tactile cues has been at the heart of research for a long time, especially for texturing (Lederman and Klatzky 2009). Yet, recent technical developments finally start to enable for virtual product manipulation, contouring and texture apprehension (Kim et al. 2013; Magnenat-Thalmann et al. 2007). As mentioned above, to date, rendering texture is enabled with friction forces or force feedback techniques (Gueorguiev et al. 2017; McGee et al. 2001) although comprehension of the haptic processing of textures through devices started about the 80s. Indeed, Lederman, Klatzky and their colleagues paved the way to explore haptic perception of texture through devices (i.e. probes versus bare fingers) from a psychophysical perspective as summarised in Table 3.2. Using either rigid probes or sheath settings for capturing texture sensations, the authors show that geometrical dimensions of texture as the spacing and the dimensions of the probes influence the psychophysical perception of

Table 3.1 Classification of tactile interfaces based on haptic rendering system

Type of interface	Tactile stimulation
Tactile feedback	Interaction by superficial mechanical actions with the skin's tactile receptors
Thermal feedback interface	Stimulation of the skin's thermal receptors
Cutaneous feedback interface	Combination of touch and thermal feedback interfaces
Motion simulation interface	Allows the modification of the orientation in space of the visualised product and to give an acceleration in rotation and/or a translation
Behavioural interfaces	A device that exploits human, natural behaviour and does not involve a significant and complex learning period in order to be used They can be divided into three categories: – Motor: device that transmits motor responses from humans to computers – Sensory: device that transmits sensory stimuli from the computer to humans – Sensor-motor: device transmitting motor responses in response to sensory stimuli sent by the computer (force feedback)

texture. The larger the space, the less the consumers detect textures, as well as when the probe diameter is larger.

Through this analysis of the literature, it becomes clear that computer sciences and consumer behaviour research have reached a crossroad regarding the interface haptic stimulation: on the one hand, the direct influence of the interface tactile cues on product, and online experiences have been acknowledged regardless of haptic rendering techniques, while, on the other hand, computer science field has been investigating for more than three decades the rendering of haptic sensations of virtual products for which the consumer behaviour research demonstrated its potential influence on further consumers' online experiences. Accordingly, the above classification from Fuchs and Moreau (2003) allows to put forward the existing and future possibilities of interface sensory capacities. However, haptic stimulation remains based on constraints detection systems in virtual environments. This means that, so far, tactile stimulation

Table 3.2 Overview of Lederman, Klatzky and their colleagues research exploring haptic perception through non-tactile rendering devices

Authors	Haptic device	Objective	Main findings
Klatzky and Lederman (1999)	Bare or covered fingers, two probes stick-like with different sizes, sheath	Evaluation of roughness of textured surfaces made of raised elements, while holding stick-like probes or through a rigid sheath mounted on the fingertip	Roughness discrimination was best with fingers although rigid links provide better discrimination for smoothest stimuli. Finally, results indicate potential viable coding of vibratory coding of roughness through rigid probes
Lederman et al. (1999)	Rigid probe	Evaluation of speed and mode of touch on roughness perception with real texture using both passive and active touch	Speed affects roughness perception via a probe
Klatzky et al. (2003b)	Bare fingers and two probes, with one eliminating force moments	Evaluation of magnitude of roughness	Importance of the probe tip diameter in relation to interelement spacing, the height of textured elements, the speed of exploration, and to a lesser extent, the type of probe

Authors	Haptic device	Objective	Main findings
Klatzky et al. (2003a)	Mouse	Evaluation of the distortion effect of visual cues on haptic guided reproduction of movement	Visual feedback distorts the haptic representation of distance used for the reproduction response
Lawrence et al. (2007)	Probes and fingers	Evaluation of perceived roughness of freely explored linear gratings with a rigid probe or finger end-effector	The groove width predicts perceived roughness evaluation in both conditions. Higher values of groove width decrease roughness perception

obtained through the device is still unrelated to the product as previous consumer research emphasises (Zhu and Meyer 2017; Brasel and Gips 2014, 2015; Shen et al. 2016). Following this assessment, the interdisciplinary research on the topic needs to consider the tangible and realistic experience provided to consumers in online environments, which is the clear next step of consumers' experience in consumption environments that become furthermore merged and almost non-dissociated in consumers' mind and perceptual processing.

3.2.2 Realism for Consumption Environments: Visual and Haptic Rendering of Texture

Historically, the idea of realism comes from Platon's doctrine according to which there are ideas, independent essences, of which individual beings and sentient things are only the reflection, the image.[3] In modern philosophy, realism is related to the independent relation between knowledge and its object. This conceptualisation is opposed to idealism, where the sense of reality is modified. From the history of literature perspective, realism is the meticulous and objective description of the facts and characters of ordinary and everyday reality. This is referred to as the "crudeness" of the action of describing. Besides, two schools of thought coexist about realism, the first of which seeks the exact resemblance to the model, while the second evokes the attitude of a person who takes reality into account and appreciates it accurately, which contrasts with unrealism. According to the Larousse[4] dictionary, realism is (1) the individual ability to see reality as it is and acts accordingly, but also represents the (2) character of what is an objective description of reality, which does not hide anything of its most raw aspects. However, research on virtual environments and technologies strongly discusses the notion of realism and its implementation. For instance, embodiment, i.e. inclusion of senses, has been widely integrated as a necessity for rendering complete user's virtual experience but does not represent a necessity for creating virtual

---

[3] https://www.cnrtl.fr/lexicographie/r%C3%A9alisme.
[4] http://www.larousse.fr/dictionnaires/francais/r%C3%A9alisme/66833?q=r%C3%A9alisme#66088.

words experiences (Biocca 1992; Fuchs and Moreau 2003). Yet McLuhan (1966) strongly suggests the inclusion of senses by defining media as "extension of the senses".

In line with this debate, in *Communication in the Age of Virtual Reality*, Heeter (1995) relates that interaction of reality and virtual reality is complex. She particularly demonstrates that one-fourth of the population is easily engaged into virtual environment, one-fourth is deeply rooted into physical reality while the rest is balanced. Accordingly, increasing the senses stimulation seems necessary but might not be enough, even though technological progress and further implementation in consumers' daily life may change the rather old percentage distribution. Nevertheless, virtual consumption and purchase will remain distinct from actual and in store as long as the full range of senses are not yet retrieved in the overall virtual reality mix (Milgram et al. 1994). Indeed, haptic rendering is still poorly engaged compared to visual integration, despite the higher potential to provide feeling of tangibility. Haptic dimension of texture still relates to the flat touchscreen tactile cues, which have an influence on consumers' judgement and behaviour (Brasel and Gips 2015). Yet, if realism is not always the aim of virtual reality environments (Heeter 1995; Fuchs and Moreau 2003), the consumption environment requires more direct connections with the physical realities that consumers know in store and daily life, particularly for tactile sensations. Therefore, tactile rendering technologies need to reproduce accurate and realistic haptic sensations through the interface to allow for product understanding and experience wherever the product and consumers are located, even though first approach of virtual environment claim for experiences and sensations more than realism which is also true for virtual experiences (Fuchs and Moreau 2006; Tikkanen et al. 2009; Haenlein and Kaplan 2009). As a result, to create furthermore realistic haptic sensations, research needs to question the concept of realism and how it is displayed in mediated environments? Most of the research on this topic notably emphasises the dual role of visual and tactile cues of computer-mediated settings to enhance product realistic perception through the stimulation of more senses.

As we know, the sense of touch is the only sense of contact enabling for tangible perception of products (see Chapter 1) while the visual sense is dominant for first product's approach (Eklund and Helmefalk 2018). Accordingly, virtual consumption has given priority to the visual sense such as visual texture rendering has come closer to reality with tools using high-definition image interactivity. For instance, the Shoogleit technology, implemented in Overmars and Poels (2015) or Blazquez Cano et al. (2017), enables consumers to fold, through the touchscreen fabrics as if folding in direct interaction. The visual representation of texture in this case increases the online perceived control and interactivity with the products as recommended by Jiang and Benbasat (2004).

In parallel, previous research on haptic rendering demonstrates that force feedback increases the sense of realism by providing tangible reactions to the consumers' actions with the product's virtual representation (Jin 2011). Considering the actual and potential effects on consumer's behaviour, haptic technologies and their afferent devices need to provide tangible- and real-world-related tactile sensations for virtual consumption such as, when a consumer grasps a product or interact with a virtual element, it is possible to feel it similarly to direct interaction (Hamilton and Thompson 2007; Daugherty et al. 2008). So far, elements as contouring, plain versus hollows, or warmth are technically possible and further integrated into daily consumers' products (Israr et al. 2014; Kim et al. 2013). Yet texture, that ultimately increases realistic manipulation, remains complex to translate into virtual environments, but technical progress slowly comes to enable it (Rekik et al. 2017; Philpott and Summers 2012). Interestingly, their findings highlight the ability of users to identify virtual textures via the device but, when it comes to compare physical and virtual textures or when more than one finger is used, consumers do not match the previously identified virtual textures with physical ones. Hence, texture rendering is complex. In particular, the difficulty relies on the anisotropy of texture that makes complicated to render in real-time conditions an identical haptic sensation of the texture as it would be in physical interaction (Philpott and Summers 2012). Anisotropy is the deformation of texture while being handled, which comprises multiple ways to end up for the product texture, and thus multiple ways to model with algorithm for texture rendering. As a result, creating such an algorithm is an ongoing challenge to overcome for engineers from a tactile perspective (HAPTEX Consortium

2008; Lin et al. 2016; Dangxiao et al. 2019). In this objective, Dadi and Hariharan (2018) recently introduced a distinctive solution for creating faster experimental research design for haptic studies with a fully adapted finger-based electro-cutaneous tactile device to simulate texture, which differs from friction stimulation also recognised to come closer to texture simulation (Rekik et al. 2017). Thus, haptic rendering for textures is an increasing research stream with promising future implementation. Yet, visual cues and development associated with these haptic sensations should lead even more to virtual texture apprehension.

From a multisensory approach, technology enables high-definition image interactivity in online consumption as we have introduced in Chapter 2. Yet, to further extend the realism of virtual consumption, the combination of both is necessary: haptic system is expert to determine material properties, particularly hardness and roughness, but vision enables to enhance tactile accuracy and is best to approach geometrical product's properties (Baumgartner et al. 2013; Klatzky et al. 1993; Li et al. 2015). Therefore, whatever the environment, the visual sense is complementary to haptic exploration (Heller 1982; Faconti et al. 2000), particularly since brain scan research have demonstrated the capacity to stimulate same tactual areas either with actual or visual-tactile stimulation (Brunyé et al. 2012; Li et al. 2015). For instance, Camillieri et al. (2018) recently demonstrated that, with friction stimulation, actual and virtual twill fabrics activated similar brain areas whereas velvety texture active very distinctive areas. In the same vein, Filip et al. (2017) proposed an efficient solution to visually improve texture apprehension for complex scenes by considering distance, which can, for example, be used in car interior exploration. Thus, tactile rendering technologies need to both satisfy visual and haptic system by enabling fast (i.e. no latency between movements for both sensory modalities), accurate (i.e. exact location) and faithful sensations which in turn will increase consumers realistic product interaction and understanding.

Tourism[5] and Fashion[6] industry, as consumption areas, particularly advanced for integrating these two parameters as both need to render

---

[5] http://www.gamification-in-tourism.com/how-to-use-virtual-reality-in-tourism/.
[6] https://fashionretail.blog/2018/05/07/ar-vr-in-fashion/.

sensory experiences to make consumers more engaged (Tussyadiah et al. 2018; tom Dieck et al. 2016; Rahman 2012; Blazquez Cano et al. 2017; Marasco et al. 2018; Guttentag 2010). In fashion retailing, high visual texture definition associated with haptic stimulation through stroking gestures on the touchscreen interfaces induces higher tactile stimulation and greater product understanding (Overmars and Poels 2015; Rahman 2012). In grocery store conditions, de Vries et al. (2018) replicated similar protocols than Brasel and Gips (2014, 2015) to further confirm the effect of interface touch on psychological ownership and endowment effect with higher image interactivity. Surprisingly, their results did not entirely support the same effects but showed that interface touch and higher image interactivity invites to more hedonic consumption consideration and behaviour. Particularly, consumers with autotelic profiles experienced better the navigation online with touchscreen interface and higher image interactivity (3D). These results, even though not new, further confirm that engineering solution needs to bring on the market solutions to enable deeper sensory stimulation based on both visual and tactual senses. Rendering technologies should satisfy the expert system of both senses to enhance the feeling of presence, immersion and interactivity in these environments and *in fine* makes the realities to be shared and consolidated (Sternberger 2006; Bouvier 2009; Sheridan 1992). The importance of considering tactile rendering with vision is highlighted in current applications in various fields that are more important than consumption only (e.g. surgery, military, etc.) (Klatzky et al. 2013).

3.3 Managerial Focus: From Imagination to Sensory Stimulation

Man has always tried to get out of his direct environment by using strategies to distract his attention from the reality in which his body evolves. Thus, imagination, stimulated by written or oral narratives, music or images, has always been the basis of this approach to extracting from the direct environment. For example, reading a novel sometimes leads the reader to feel the hero's experiences. However, a normal individual is aware that this experience is lived only by proxy and keeps his distance from fiction: it will therefore not be considered as her/his reality. Indeed, to include an experience in her/his reality, one needs to feel its materiality through her/his senses. It is no longer an experience simply suggested to our brain by evocation, but an experience partially lived by our sensory sensors. For example, visualising an adventure film in 3 dimensions leads us to visualise the danger on the screen as if it was really facing us or to hear the sounds of the story on either side of our body "as if we were there".

Therefore, researchers have long identified the need to stimulate the five senses in accordance with an evocation to reinforce the impression of reality of the lived experience. The most famous example of this approach is the Sensorama. In 1955, film-maker Morton Heilig began developing a multisensory device to provide a complete virtual experience. After a few years of work, he presented a functional prototype in 1962, the Sensorama. This entirely mechanical device looks like a large arcade bollard. It consists of a chair simulating movement, a wide-angle stereoscopic screen and stereo speakers. It even has a wind tunnel to recreate the effects of the wind and a perfume diffuser. Too far ahead of its time, the Sensorama did not convince the investors of the time and was never commercialised.

Subsequently, experiments aimed at immersing individuals in virtual experiences have prioritised one or two sensory stimuli, abandoning the idea of operationalising a solution as complete as the Sensorama. The simple example of the role of music in a meditation class that allows participants to imagine themselves in a peaceful place illustrates that a one-sensory stimulation can be immersive. As another example, 3-D home cinema is based on a sense of sight and sound that gives the illusion that the action taking place on the screen is located close to the physical environment. Gradually, the leisure industry is trying to produce the most complete sensory experience possible using technological developments. For example, Kinepolis cinemas in Belgium rely on 4DX technology which, according to its manager "raises cinema to a four-dimensional level: spectators are no longer content to watch a film, they are an integral part of the action. The moving seats and atmospheric effects (including wind, water, water, odours and light) perfectly synchronised with what happens on the screen, ensure a totally new immersive cinematic experience that appeals to all senses".

3.4 Conclusion

With the fast evolution of interfaces, the issue for realism in virtual environments is probably a matter of time before consumers become enough used to mediated consumption or that interfaces become transparent enough to make the consumption environment one and only instead of distinct dimensions. Therefore, sensory input from virtual environments, that are different, will soon become natural sensations due to human psychological learning and biology adaptation (Kock 2004).

In Chapter 2, we discussed how business and engineers have given interest to the visual cues to compensate with the absence of haptic stimulation in online environments by creating high image interactivity technologies with fine visual product definition, often completed with auditory cues. In this chapter, we further developed the discussion by showing how tactile cues of the interfaces also influence consumers' online consumption experiences even though these are not always related to the product tactile cues. We also showed that tactile rendering technologies influence consumers' haptic perception such as it provides further tangibility. Finally, technology is increasingly growing towards haptic stimulation that relates to the product tactile cues, either geometrical or material to provide the full sensory experience described by pioneer as Heilig in the 1950s or Sutherland (1965). Therefore, in a near future, consumers should be able to feel products and use their haptic system to obtain diagnostic and fun experiences. We discuss these future possibilities in Chapter 4 by introducing original experiments and extrapolate for future research and potential haptic experience in consumption environments.

References

Allerkamp, Dennis, Guido Böttcher, Franz Erich Wolter, Alan C. Brady, Jianguo Qu, and Ian R. Summers. 2007. "A Vibrotactile Approach to Tactile Rendering." *Visual Computer* 23 (2): 97–108. https://doi.org/10.1007/s00371-006-0031-5.

Barsalou, Lawrence W. 1999. "Perceptual Symbol System." *Behavioral and Brain Sciences* 22: 577–660. https://doi.org/10.1098/rstb.2003.1319.

———. 2003. "Abstraction in Perceptual Symbol Systems." *Philosophical Transactions of the Royal Society B: Biological Sciences* 358 (1435): 1177–87. https://doi.org/10.1098/rstb.2003.1319.

———. 2008. "Grounded Cognition." *Annual Review of Psychology* 59 (1): 617–45. https://doi.org/10.1146/annurev.psych.59.103006.093639.

Baumgartner, Elisabeth, Christiane B. Wiebel, and Karl R. Gegenfurtner. 2013. "Visual and Haptic Representations of Material Properties." *Multisensory Research* 26 (5): 429–55. https://doi.org/10.1163/22134808-00002429.

Biocca, Frank. 1992. "Virtual Reality Technology: A Tutorial." *Journal of Communication* 42 (4): 23–72. https://doi.org/10.1111/j.1460-2466.1992.tb00811.x.

Blazquez Cano, Marta, Patsy Perry, Rachel Ashman, and Kathryn Waite. 2017. "The Influence of Image Interactivity upon User Engagement When Using Mobile Touch Screens." *Computers in Human Behavior* 77: 406–12. https://doi.org/10.1016/j.chb.2017.03.042.

Bouvier, Patrice. 2009. "La Présence En Réalité Virtuelle, Une Approche Centrée Utilisateur." Université Paris-Est.

Brasel, S. Adam, and James Gips. 2014. "Tablets, Touchscreens, and Touchpads: How Varying Touch Interfaces Trigger Psychological Ownership and Endowment." *Journal of Consumer Psychology* 24 (2): 226–33. https://doi.org/10.1016/j.jcps.2013.10.003.

———. 2015. "Interface Psychology: Touchscreens Change Attribute Importance, Decision Criteria, and Behavior in Online Choice." *Cyberpsychology, Behavior, and Social Networking* 18 (9): 534–38. https://doi.org/10.1089/cyber.2014.0546.

Brunyé, Tad T., Eliza K. Walters, Tali Ditman, Stephanie A. Gagnon, Caroline R. Mahoney, and Holly A. Taylor. 2012. "The Fabric of Thought: Priming Tactile Properties During Reading Influences Direct Tactile Perception." *Cognitive Science* 36 (8): 1449–67. https://doi.org/10.1111/j.1551-6709.2012.01268.x.

Camillieri, Brigitte, Marie Ange Bueno, Marie Fabre, Benjamin Juan, Betty Lemaire-Semail, and Laurence Mouchnino. 2018. "From Finger Friction and Induced Vibrations to Brain Activation: Tactile Comparison Between Real and Virtual Textile Fabrics." *Tribology International* 126 (May): 283–96. https://doi.org/10.1016/j.triboint.2018.05.031.

Childers, Terry L., Christopher L. Carr, Joann Peck, and Stephen Carson. 2001. "Hedonic and Utilitarian Motivations for Online Retail Shopping Behavior." *Journal of Retailing* 77 (4): 511–35.

Chung, Sorim, Thomas Kramer, and Elaine M. Wong. 2018. "Do Touch Interface Users Feel More Engaged? The Impact of Input Device Type on Online Shoppers' Engagement, Affect, and Purchase Decisions." *Psychology and Marketing* 35 (11): 795–806. https://doi.org/10.1002/mar.21135.

Citrin, Alka Varma, Donald E. Stem, Eric R. Spangenberg, and Michael J. Clark. 2003. "Consumer Need for Tactile Input: An Internet Retailing Challenge." *Journal of Business Research* 56 (11): 915–22. https://doi.org/10.1016/S0148-2963(01)00278-8.

Dadi, Ravikanth, and P. Hariharan. 2018. "Design of Electrocutaneous Tactile Display over Human Fingertip for Textural Applications in Space Manufacturing Feedback." *Procedia Computer Science* 133: 684–90. https://doi.org/10.1016/j.procs.2018.07.131.

Dangxiao, Wang, Guo Yuan, Liu Shiyi, Zhang Yuru, Xu Weiliang, and Xiao Jing. 2019. "Haptic Display for Virtual Reality: Progress and Challenges." *Virtual Reality & Intelligent Hardware* 1 (2): 136. https://doi.org/10.3724/sp.j.2096-5796.2019.0008.

Daugherty, Terry, Hairong Li, and Frank Biocca. 2008. "Consumer Learning and the Effects of Virtual Experience Relative to Indirect and Direct Product Experience." *Psychology & Marketing* 25 (7): 568–86. https://doi.org/10.1002/mar.20225.

Debrégeas, Georges, Alexis Prevost, and Julien Scheibert. 2009. "Toucher Digital Humain: Transduction Mécanique de l'information Tactile et Rôle Des Empreintes Digitales." *Images de La Physique*, 11–17.

de Vries, Rachelle, Gerry Jager, Irene Tijssen, and Elizabeth H. Zandstra. 2018. "Shopping for Products in a Virtual World: Why Haptics and Visuals Are Equally Important in Shaping Consumer Perceptions and Attitudes." *Food Quality and Preference* 66 (June): 64–75. https://doi.org/10.1016/j.foodqual.2018.01.005.

Eklund, Andreas Aldogan, and Miralem Helmefalk. 2018. "Seeing Through Touch: A Conceptual Framework of Visual-Tactile Interplay." *Journal of Product and Brand Management* 27 (5): 498–513. https://doi.org/10.1108/JPBM-07-2017-1520.

Faconti, G., M. Massink, M. Bordegoni, F. De Angelis, and S. Booth. 2000. "Haptic Cues for Image Disambiguation." *Computer Graphics Forum* 19 (3): C-169–C-178. http://www.scopus.

com/inward/record.url?eid=2-s2.0-0343338124&partnerID=40&md5= 48ed5c82589e0f3d691675e3454dabc9.

Filip, J., R. Vávra, M. Havlíček, and M. Krupička. 2017. "Predicting Visual Perception of Material Structure in Virtual Environments." *Computer Graphics Forum* 36 (1): 89–100. https://doi.org/10.1111/cgf.12789.

Flavián, Carlos, Sergio Ibáñez-Sánchez, and Carlos Orús. 2019. "The Impact of Virtual, Augmented and Mixed Reality Technologies on the Customer Experience." *Journal of Business Research* 100 (October): 547–60. https://doi.org/10.1016/j.jbusres.2018.10.050.

Fuchs, Philippe, and Guillaume Moreau. 2003. *Le Traité de La Réalité Virtuelle - Fondements et Interfaces Comportementales*. Edited by Philippe Fuchs and Guillaume Moreau. Paris: Presse de.

———. 2006. *Le Traité de La Réalité Virtuelle - Création Des Environnements Virtuels & Applications*. Edited by Philippe Fuchs and Guillaume Moreau. Paris: Presse de.

Giebelhausen, Michael, Stacy G. Robinson, Nancy J. Sirianni, and Michael K. Brady. 2014. "Touch vs. Tech: When Technology Functions as a Barrier or a Benefit to Service Encounters." *Journal of Marketing* 78 (July): 113–24. http://journals.ama.org/doi/abs/10.1509/jm.13.0056.

Gleckman, H. 2000. "Buying Clothes Online: Color Me Jaded." *BusinessWeek Online*, May 1.

Grundwald, Martin. 2008. *Human Haptic Perception, Basic and Applications*. Edited by Martin Grundwald. Berlin: Birkhäuser.

Gueorguiev, David, Eric Vezzoli, André Mouraux, Betty Lemaire-Semail, and Jean Louis Thonnard. 2017. "The Tactile Perception of Transient Changes in Friction." *Journal of the Royal Society Interface* 14 (137). https://doi.org/10.1098/rsif.2017.0641.

Guttentag, Daniel A. 2010. "Virtual Reality: Applications and Implications for Tourism." *Tourism Management* 31 (5): 637–51. https://doi.org/10.1016/j.tourman.2009.07.003.

Haans, Antal, Renske de Bruijn, and Wijnand A. IJsselsteijn. 2014. "A Virtual Midas Touch? Touch, Compliance, and Confederate Bias in Mediated Communication." *Journal of Nonverbal Behavior* 38 (3): 301–11. https://doi.org/10.1007/s10919-014-0184-2.

Haenlein, Michael, and A. M. Kaplan. 2009. "Les Magasins de Marques Phares Dans Les Mondes Virtuels: L'impact de l'exposition Au Magasin Virtuel Sur l'attitude Envers La Marque et l'intention d'achat Dans La Vie." *Recherche et Applications En Marketing* 24 (3): 57–80. http://ram.sagepub.com/content/24/3/57.short.

Hamilton, Rebecca W., and Debora Viana Thompson. 2007. "Is There a Substitute for Direct Experience? Comparing Consumers' Preferences After Direct and Indirect Product Experiences." *Journal of Consumer Research* 34 (December): 546–55.

HAPTEX Consortium. 2008. "Whole Haptic Interface: Report on the Development Activities." *HAPTEX Deliverable D4.3*, 36. http://haptex.miralab.unige.ch/.

Hardey, Mariann. 2011. "Generation C: Content, Creation, Connections and Choice." *International Journal of Market Research* 53 (6): 749. https://doi.org/10.2501/IJMR-53-6-749-770.

Heeter, Carrie. 1995. "Communication Research on Consumer VR." In *Communication in the Age of Virtual Reality*, edited by Frank Biocca and Mark Levy, 191–218. Hillsdale, NJ: Lawrence Erlbaum Associates.

Heller, Morton A. 1982. "Visual and Tactual Texture Perception: Intersensory Cooperation." *Perception & Psychophysics* 31 (4): 339–44. https://doi.org/10.3758/bf03202657.

Hoffman, Donna L., and Thomas P. Novak. 1996. "Marketing in Hypermedia Computer-Mediated Environments: Conceptual Foundations." *Journal of Marketing* 60 (3): 50. https://doi.org/10.2307/1251841.

Hoffmann, Christian Pieter, Christoph Lutz, and Miriam Meckel. 2014. "Digital Natives or Digital Immigrants? The Impact of User Characteristics on Online Trust." *Journal of Management Information Systems* 31 (3): 138–71. https://doi.org/10.1080/07421222.2014.995538.

Israr, Ali, Siyan Zhao, Kaitlyn Schwalje, Roberta Klatzky, and Jill Lehman. 2014. "Feel Effects: Enriching Storytelling with Haptic Feedback." *ACM Transactions on Applied Perception* 1 (1): 1–17.

Jiang, Zhenhui, and Izak Benbasat. 2004. "Virtual Product Experience: Effects of Visual and Functional Control of Products on Perceived Diagnosticity and Flow in Electronic Shopping." *Journal of Management Information Systems* 21 (3): 111–47. https://doi.org/10.1080/07421222.2004.11045817.

Jin, Seung-A Annie. 2011. "The Impact of 3D Virtual Haptics in Marketing." *Psychology and Marketing* 28 (3): 240–55. https://doi.org/10.1002/mar.20390.

Joiner, Richard, Jeff Gavin, Mark Brosnan, John Cromby, Helen Gregory, Jane Guiller, Pam Maras, and Amy Moon. 2013. "Comparing First and Second Generation Digital Natives' Internet Use, Internet Anxiety, and Internet Identification." *Cyberpsychology, Behavior and Social Networking* 16 (7): 549–52. https://doi.org/10.1089/cyber.2012.0526.

Kim, Seung-Chan, Ali Israr, and Ivan Poupyrev. 2013. "Tactile Rendering of 3D Features on Touch Surfaces." *Proceedings of the 26th Annual ACM Symposium on User Interface Software and Technology—UIST '13*, 531–38. https://doi.org/10.1145/2501988.2502020.

Klatzky, Roberta L., and Susan J. Lederman. 1999. "Tactile Roughness Perception with a Rigid Link Interposed Between Skin and Surface." *Perception & Psychophysics* 61 (4): 591–607. https://doi.org/10.3758/BF03205532.

Klatzky, Roberta L., S. J. Lederman, and D. E. Matula. 1993. "Haptic Exploration in the Presence of Vision." *Journal of Experimental Psychology: Human Perception and Performance* 19 (4): 726–43.

Klatzky, Roberta L., Susan J. Lederman, and Sara Langseth. 2003a. "Watching a Cursor Distorts Haptically Guided Reproduction of Mouse Movement." *Journal of Experimental Psychology: Applied* 9 (4): 228–35. https://doi.org/10.1037/1076-898X.9.4.228.

Klatzky, Roberta L., Susan J. Lederman, Cheryl Hamilton, Molly Grindley, and Robert H. Swendsen. 2003b. "Feeling Textures Through a Probe: Effects of Probe and Surface Geometry and Exploratory Factors." *Perception & Psychophysics* 65 (4): 613–31. https://doi.org/10.3758/BF03194587.

Klatzky, Roberta L., Dianne Pawluk, and Angelika Peer. 2013. "Haptic Perception of Material Properties and Implications for Applications." *Proceedings of the IEEE* (99): 1–12. https://doi.org/10.1109/JPROC.2013.2248691.

Kock, Ned. 2004. "The Psychobiological Model: Towards a New Theory of Computer-Mediated Communication Based on Darwinian Evolution." *Organization Science* 15 (3): 327–48. https://doi.org/10.1287/orsc.1040.0071.

———. 2005. "Media Richness or Media Naturalness? The Evolution of Our Biological Communication Apparatus and Its Influence on Our Behavior Toward E-Communication Tools." *IEEE Transactions on Professional Communication* 48 (2): 117–30. https://doi.org/10.1109/TPC.2005.849649.

Lawrence, Michael A., Ryo Kitada, Roberta L. Klatzky, and Susan J. Lederman. 2007. "Haptic Roughness Perception of Linear Gratings via Bare Finger or Rigid Probe." *Perception* 36 (4): 547–57. https://doi.org/10.1068/p5746.

Laycock, S. D., and A. M. Day. 2007. "A Survey of Haptic Rendering Techniques." *Computer Graphics Forum* 26 (1): 50–65. https://doi.org/10.1111/j.1467-8659.2007.00945.x.

Lederman, Susan J., and Roberta L. Klatzky. 2009. "Haptic Perception: A Tutorial." *Attention, Perception & Psychophysics* 71 (7): 1439–59. https://doi.org/10.3758/APP.71.7.1439.

Lederman, S. J., R. L. Klatzky, C. L. Hamilton, and G. I. Ramsay. 1999. "Perceiving Roughness via a Rigid Probe: Psychophysical Effects of Exploration Speed and Mode of Touch." *Haptics-E* 1: 1–20. https://doi.org/99.1999/lederman.haptics-e.

Li, Min, Jelizaveta Konstantinova, Emanuele L. Secco, Allen Jiang, Hongbin Liu, Thrishantha Nanayakkara, Lakmal D. Seneviratne, Prokar Dasgupta, Kaspar Althoefer, and Helge A. Wurdemann. 2015. "Using Visual Cues to Enhance Haptic Feedback for Palpation on Virtual Model of Soft Tissue." *Medical and Biological Engineering and Computing* 53 (11): 1177–86. https://doi.org/10.1007/s11517-015-1309-4.

Lin, Ting Hao, Der Lor Way, Zen Chung Shih, Wen Kai Tai, and Chin Chen Chang. 2016. "An Efficient Structure-Aware Bilateral Texture Filtering for Image Smoothing." *Computer Graphics Forum* 35 (7): 57–66. https://doi.org/10.1111/cgf.13003.

Magnenat-Thalmann, Nadia, P. Volino, U. Bonanni, Ian R. Summers, M. Bergamasco, F. Salsedo, and Franz-Erich Wolter. 2007. "From Physics-Based Simulation to the Touching of Textiles: The HAPTEX Project." *International Journal of Virtual Reality* 6 (3): 35–44.

Marasco, Alessandra, Piera Buonincontri, Mathilda van Niekerk, Marissa Orlowski, and Fevzi Okumus. 2018. "Exploring the Role of Next-Generation Virtual Technologies in Destination Marketing." *Journal of Destination Marketing and Management* 9 (January): 138–48. https://doi.org/10.1016/j.jdmm.2017.12.002.

McCabe, Deborah Brown, and Stephen M. Nowlis. 2003. "The Effect of Examining Actual Products or Product Descriptions on Consumer Preference." *Journal of Consumer Psychology* 13 (4): 431–39. https://doi.org/10.1207/S15327663JCP1304_10.

McGee, Marilyn Rose, Philip Gray, and Stephen Brewster. 2001. "Haptic Perception of Virtual Roughness." In *CHI '01 Extended Abstracts on Human Factors in Computer Systems—CHI '01*, 155. New York, NY: ACM Press. https://doi.org/10.1145/634158.634162.

McLuhan, M. 1966. *Understanding Media*. New York: Signet.

Milgram, Paul, Haruo Takemura, Akira Utsumi, and Fumio Kishino. 1994. "Augmented Reality: A Class of Displays on the Reality-Virtuality Continuum." In *Telemanipulator and Telepresence Technologies*, edited by Hari Das, 2351, 282–92. https://doi.org/10.1117/12.197321.

Mulcahy, Rory Francis, and Aimee S. Riedel. 2018. "'Touch It, Swipe It, Shake It': Does the Emergence of Haptic Touch in Mobile Retailing Advertising

Improve Its Effectiveness?" *Journal of Retailing and Consumer Services* (May): 0–1. https://doi.org/10.1016/j.jretconser.2018.05.011.

Overmars, Suzanne, and Karolien Poels. 2015. "Online Product Experiences: The Effect of Simulating Stroking Gestures on Product Understanding and the Critical Role of User Control." *Computers in Human Behavior* 51 (Part A): 272–84. https://doi.org/10.1016/j.chb.2015.04.033.

Pagani, Margherita, Margot Racat, and Charles F. Hofacker. 2019. "Adding Voice to the Omnichannel and How That Affects Brand Trust." *Journal of Interactive Marketing* 48: 89–105. https://doi.org/10.1016/j.intmar.2019.05.002.

Parisi, David. 2014. "Reach In and Feel Something: On the Strategic Reconstruction of Touch in Virtual Space." *Animation: An Interdisciplinary Journal* 9 (2): 228–44. https://doi.org/10.1177/1746847714527195.

———. 2018. *Archaeologies of Touch: Interfacing with Haptics from Electricity to Computing*. Minneapolis: University of Minnesota Press.

Peck, Joann, and T. L. Childers. 2003b. "To Have and to Hold: The Influence of Haptic Information on Product Judgments." *Journal of Marketing* 67 (2): 35–48.

Philpott, Matthew, and Ian R. Summers. 2012. "Evaluating a Multipoint Tactile Renderer for Virtual Textured Surfaces." *Proceedings of Eurohaptics 2012*, 121–26.

Racat, Margot. 2016. "L'influence de La Stimulation Tactile Lors de l'évaluation En Ligne d'un Produit." University of Lyon.

Racat, Margot, and Sonia Capelli. 2016. "L'impact de La Similarité Sur l'efficacité Des Outils d'aide à La Vente En Ligne." *Revue Francaise de Gestion* 254 (1): 89–105. https://doi.org/10.3166/rfg.2016.00005.

Rahman, Osmud. 2012. "The Influence of Visual and Tactile Inputs on Denim Jeans Evaluation." *International Journal of Design* 6 (1): 11–24.

Rekik, Yosra, Eric Vezzoli, and Laurent Grisoni. 2017. "Understanding Users' Perception of Simultaneous Tactile Textures," September, 1–6. https://doi.org/10.1145/3098279.3098528.

Robles-De-La-Torre, Gabriel. 2008. "Principles of Haptic Perception in Virtual Environments." In *Human Haptic Perception: Basics and Applications*, 363–79. Basel: Birkhäuser Basel. https://doi.org/10.1007/978-3-7643-7612-3_30.

Salisbury, K., D. Brock, T. Massie, N. Swarup, and C. Zilles. 1995. "Haptic Rendering." In *Proceedings of the 1995 Symposium on Interactive 3D Graphics—SI3D '95*, 123–30. New York, NY: ACM Press. https://doi.org/10.1145/199404.199426.

Schlosser, A. E. 2006. "Learning Through Virtual Product Experience: The Role of Imagery on True Versus False Memories." *Journal of Consumer Research* 33 (3): 377–83. https://doi.org/10.1086/508522.

Shen, Hao, Meng Zhang, and Aradhna Krishna. 2016. "Computer Interfaces and the 'Direct-Touch' Effect: Can IPads Increase the Choice of Hedonic Food?" *Journal of Marketing Research* 53 (5): 745–58.

Sheridan, Thomas B. 1992. "Musings on Telepresence and Virtual Presence." *Presence: Teleoperators and Virtual Environments* 1 (1): 120–26. https://doi.org/10.1162/pres.1992.1.1.120.

Skedung, Lisa, Katrin Danerlöv, Ulf Olofsson, Carl Michael Johannesson, Maiju Aikala, John Kettle, Martin Arvidsson, Birgitta Berglund, and Mark W. Rutland. 2011. "Tactile Perception: Finger Friction, Surface Roughness and Perceived Coarseness." *Tribology International* 44 (5): 505–12.

Spence, Charles, and A. Gallace. 2011. "Multisensory Design: Reaching Out to Touch the Consumer." *Psychology & Marketing* 28 (3): 267–308.

Sternberger, M. Ludovic. 2006. "Interaction En Réalité Virtuelle." Université Louis Pasteur de Strasbourg 1.

Steuer, Jonathan. 1992. "Defining Virtual Reality: Dimensions Determining Telepresence." *Journal of Communication* 42 (4): 73–93. https://doi.org/10.1111/j.1460-2466.1992.tb00812.x.

Sutherland, Ivan E. 1965. "The Ultimate Display." *Proceedings of the Congress of the International Federation of Information Processing (IFIP)*, 506–8. https://doi.org/10.1109/MC.2005.274.

Tikkanen, Henrikki, Joel Hietanen, Tuomas Henttonen, and Joonas Rokka. 2009. "Exploring Virtual Worlds: Success Factors in Virtual World Marketing." *Management Decision* 47 (8): 1357–81.

tom Dieck, M. Claudia, Timothy Jung, and Dai In Han. 2016. "Mapping Requirements for the Wearable Smart Glasses Augmented Reality Museum Application." *Journal of Hospitality and Tourism Technology* 7 (3): 230–53. https://doi.org/10.1108/JHTT-09-2015-0036.

Tussyadiah, Iis P., Timothy Hyungsoo Jung, and M. Claudia tom Dieck. 2018. "Embodiment of Wearable Augmented Reality Technology in Tourism Experiences." *Journal of Travel Research* 57 (5): 597–611. https://doi.org/10.1177/0047287517709090.

Unger, Bertram, Ralph Hollis, and Roberta Klatzky. 2011. "Roughness Perception in Virtual Textures." *IEEE Transactions on Haptics* 4 (2): 122–33. https://doi.org/10.1109/TOH.2010.61.

Varadarajan, Rajan, Raji Srinivasan, Gautham Gopal Vadakkepatt, Manjit S. Yadav, Paul A. Pavlou, Sandeep Krishnamurthy, and Tom Krause. 2010. "Interactive Technologies and Retailing Strategy: A Review, Conceptual Framework and Future Research Directions." *Journal of Interactive Marketing* 24 (2): 96–110. https://doi.org/10.1016/j.intmar.2010.02.004.

Verhoef, Peter C., Andrew T. Stephen, P. K. Kannan, Xueming Luo, Vibhanshu Abhishek, Michelle Andrews, Yakov Bart, H. Datta, N. Fong, D. L. Hoffman, and M. M. Hu. 2017. "Consumer Connectivity in a Complex, Technology-Enabled, and Mobile-Oriented World with Smart Products." *Journal of Interactive Marketing* 40: 1–8. https://doi.org/10.1016/j.intmar.2017.06.001.

Vermeulen, Nicolas, Olivier Corneille, and Paula M. Niedenthal. 2008. "Sensory Load Incurs Conceptual Processing Costs." *Cognition* 109 (2): 287–94. https://doi.org/10.1016/j.cognition.2008.09.004.

Yadav, Manjit S., and Paul A. Pavlou. 2014. "Marketing in Computer-Mediated Environments: Research Synthesis and New Directions." *Journal of Marketing* 78 (1): 20–40. https://doi.org/10.1509/jm.12.0020.

Zeng, Tao, Frédéric Giraud, Betty Lemaire-Semail, and Michel Amberg. 2010. "Analysis of a New Haptic Display Coupling Tactile and Kinesthetic Feedback to Render Texture and Shape." *Lecture Notes in Computer Science (Including Subseries Lecture Notes in Artificial Intelligence and Lecture Notes in Bioinformatics)* 6192 LNCS (Part 2): 87–93. https://doi.org/10.1007/978-3-642-14075-4_13.

Zhu, Ying, and Jeffrey Meyer. 2017. "Getting in Touch with Your Thinking Style: How Touchscreens Influence Purchase." *Journal of Retailing and Consumer Services* 38 (September): 51–58. https://doi.org/10.1016/j.jretconser.2017.05.006.

4

The Future of Consumption in a Haptic-Based World

Abstract This chapter aims to provide a set of research with specifics examples that support the development of the previous chapters. It particularly focuses on recent and relevant research on haptic interfaces (development and consumer approach) as well as it will develop a first-hand research study with materials that lies down the foundation to consider for future haptic interface in consumption.

Keywords Sensory similarity · Congruence · Texture · Perception · Experiment

This chapter aims to provide a set of research with specifics examples that support the development of the previous chapters. It particularly focuses on recent and relevant research on haptic interfaces (development and consumer approach) as well as it will develop a first-hand research study with materials that lies down the foundation to consider for future haptic interface in consumption.

4.1 To Mimic or Not to Mimic the Reality? That Is the Question

Parisi (2018a, p. 238) reports that "with the extension of touch across space facilitated by new tactile interfaces, [...] human bodies would no longer need to travel; the distant material world could be rendered as computer code and then reconstructed by touch interface, thereby eliminating the need to move bodies through space". This assumption stands for a long time in the imaginary of the virtual reality system. Indeed, as we emphasised in previous chapters, the role of sensory stimulation is at the core of the development of digital interfaces to render full and real-based experiences from the consumer perspective. So far, past literature has not investigated the physiological and psychological mechanism related to the interfaces as being part of the whole experience that triggers senses and perceptual systems. Thus, previously we highlighted the lack of interest for questioning the relationship between the sensory stimulation provided by the interface and the one provided by the offer presented on the screen. Here, we suggest to precisely address the question with a focus on texture assessment via visual (offer presented on the screen) and tactile interaction (tactile rendering provided by the interface).

We introduce two studies based on experimental methodology to provide insights on the underlying psychological mechanism that occurs through physiological stimulation. The first study investigates the consumer's need for the online purchase experience to mimic the real purchase experience. Therefore, we compared buyers testing make-up products with real testers with buyers using a virtual try-on interface. The second study investigates more precisely the interaction effect between the texture of the product presented on the screen of the interface and the tactile rendering of this interface. In others words, we search whether online buyers are looking for realistic tactile sensations—a tactile sensation congruent with the visual texture of the product—or if they are simply looking for fun, valorising the tactile rendering as such, without connection with the visual texture of the product presented on the screen. The results further extend previous work that give interest to the role of the touch-based interfaces as hedonic/experiential or utilitarian/rational lever for online consumption and further complement the psychological endowment effect previously shown (Brasel and Gips 2014, 2015; Zhu and Meyer 2017; Shen et al. 2016) but demonstrating other psychological mechanisms that comes from the perceptual system.

4.1.1 Congruency and Similarity in Mediated Environments

In Chapter 3, we reviewed the different conception and utility of realism from virtual reality engineers and consumption perspectives. Based on the literature, we concluded that realistic condition for virtual interaction is necessary for the consumer to believe that what is done is real and has consequences on his or her own environment, even though the actions and results might be completely virtual-based. Furthermore, we positioned that sensory information processing is based on the theory of grounded cognition which allows to consider the perceptual systems to be integrated into the information processing understanding (Barsalou 1999, 2010). As such, we further consider that psychological processing as congruency is relevant for understanding mediated consumption through interfaces but not enough with regard to the sensory information processing. As mentioned before, the senses do not make any difference between the physical and virtual environments since it only considers what is "at hand" (Montagu 1971). Indeed, sensory perception is recognised to be the first step to capture and identify information and then be transmitted and captured into a mental conception (Grunwald 2008; Barsalou 1999). Therefore, the mental processing of the different information allows for the dissociation between environments and tells the senses that touch is related to the interface while the visual sense sees the product through the interface. From a consumer perspective, people tend to better understand the online and indirect product manipulation when it shares similar sensory cues with the same direct product manipulation (i.e. in-store versus 3D online product examination). De facto, the concept of similarity is central when it comes to perception and cognition sciences (Taylor and Hummel 2007). Accordingly, we proposed to review both concepts of congruence and similarity, show their limitations with regard to the sensory processing of information and then introduce a refine that we labelled *sensory similarity*.

Congruency is the concept that best reflects the way consumers interact with product in mediated environment such as they tend to create inference on their previous knowledge about the product and what they observe on the screen to find relational associations and thus interpret and evaluate. In marketing literature, congruency refers to the fact that "two entities (or more) fit well together" and is interchangeably used with the terms *congruity, congruence or congruent* (Fleck and Maille 2010). Congruency is a cognitive concept that uses one's experience and previous knowledge to evaluate a situation or a product. Overall, congruency is a complex concept according to Fleck and Maille (2010) which mostly refers to the discontinuity and the rupture between two things. Its complexity is due to the lack of semantic common ground and clearer delimitation of the concept. For instance, congruency is reflected with three main conceptions in the marketing literature: the relevance (Aaker and Keller 1990; Park et al. 1991), the compliance with expectation (Meyers-Levy and Tybout 1989; Dimofte et al. 2003) and the last one that gathers both relevancy and expectation (Goodman 1980; Heckler and Childers 1992). Thus, definition of the concept remains unclear and scarce with regard to its large use in the literature, in particular with equivalent terms as *fit, appropriateness, match-up, relatedness, suitability, etc.,* which have no clear definition associated with congruency (Maille and Fleck 2011, p. 79). In most cases, congruency is not defined and rather stated as being or not for further hypothesis testing. For a complete review of the concept, the interested reader might consider to read both Fleck and Maille (2010) and Maille and Fleck (2011). Moreover, in their considerable work, the authors also underline the absence of clearer definition and measure of the concept of similarity that shares common ground with congruency on the cognitive level but rather differ when it comes to more sensorial considerations.

On this matter, the concept of similarity has been defined through a dual conception labelled the *literal* and *relational* similarity: on the one hand, it refers to the physical relations that exist between two objects (i.e. physical cues), and, on the other hand, it refers to the relational aspect that exists between the objects and products (Gentner and Gunn 2001), which is closer to congruency. *Similarity* has been discussed in the literature as a global phenomenon or as a component of cognitive processes (i.e. categorisations, memory process, decision-making, etc.) (Sagi et al. 2012; Bèzes and Mercanti-Guérin 2016). Yet in these conceptions, *similarity* has been reduced to the tangible aspects of the product attributes whereas sensory perception does not only rely on these two. Indeed, among the first consideration of *similarity*, Tversky and Gati (1978), through their contrast model, showed that it is not a unitary concept and used the physical attributes of the objects. Heit (1997) defined similarity as "*an increasing function of common features, that is features in common to the two objects and as a decreasing function of distinctive features, that is features that apply to one object but not the other*". Yet it rather relies on a variety of similarity relations, which has also been underlined by Goodman (1980) who argued that the concept of similarity is not theoretically viable since it varies and is relative to the context or the objects. In contrast, Shepard (1964) and Torgerson (1965) demonstrated that, even though the relativeness and variability, it follows a regular path, but they position the similarity as a mental distance mainly. Consequently, we propose to focus on the sensory cues and to refine the concept of similarity through a third conceptual consideration which is the concept of *sensory similarity*.

As previously introduced, knowledge is first shaped by sensory perceptions of the body and then transformed and analysed in the brain by neuronal interactions (i.e. cognitive process) (Barsalou 2008). Rosa and Malter (2003) explained that embodied cognition is constrained by physical interactions with a product because body sensors deliver information that is translated to the brain as a mental representation, that is embodied representation. For instance, an individual who physically manipulates a bath towel gathers information about the towel through the sense of touch, which he or she then cognitively interprets to evaluate the towel's comfort or softness (Grohmann et al. 2007). So, based on the embodied cognition theory and based on Montagu (1971), the senses do not make differences between two environments. It is our ability to cognitively make a difference that will make us understand that a difference exists between the two types of sensory perception due to the mediation process of the environment. If we consider only the information acquisition processing, any organs, and particularly the sense of touch, are unable to make a difference to "tell" whether the sensation comes from a direct or indirect environment since the sensation perceived is, in any case, a "direct" sensory perception. It is only through our cognitive processing that we come to make a differentiation between the sensations perceived through one environment to another, meaning what "should" be perceived in the "real" environment. For this reason, we believe that the current conception of similarity is not accurate from a sensory perspective. Even though it does come closer compared to congruency to the conceptualisation of the knowledge and information acquisition processing, it, however, remains cognitively based. Thus, we consider the concept of similarity that we sharpen to the concept of *sensory similarity,* such as we define sensory similarity in online purchase context as *the extent to which an indirect, online sensory experience of a product mimics a direct, in-store sensory experience of this product.* Compared to the cognitive perspective, the concept of sensory similarity considers both the sensory and cognitive part of knowledge and information acquisition, which will then lead to form a global perception and understanding of the product.

Regarding the mediated environments, research has not, so far, considered the relation between the interface tactile modalities and the product tactile cues. Yet, based on our conceptualisation, we assume that there is an interaction from a tactile perspective on consumers' online product evaluation. When a consumer's online product manipulation experience is similar to a direct tactile product experience, the consumer is likely to value the examined product more highly (Daugherty et al. 2008). Just as, we specifically search for understanding how the texture of an interface, sharing sensory cues with the product texture, influences consumers' behaviour, since technology is coming further on this ground (Parisi and Archer 2017; Parisi 2018a; Gueorguiev et al. 2017; Unger et al. 2011). We suggest that the device used by the consumer to purchase a product should stimulate the sense of touch to reproduce, as closely as possible, the physical experience of examining the product by hand. To enhance sensory similarity, there should be congruency between the tactile cues of the interface and the tactile cues of the product visualised on screen. For instance, research on online product manipulation showed that the more vivid and interactive the experience, the more the consumer perceived the online product manipulation to be analogue to a real product manipulation (Jiang and Benbasat 2004; Brasel and Gips 2015, 2014). Therefore, we contend that informational tactile stimulation—by which a device provides tactile cues about the product (i.e. congruency of texture)—should increase sensory similarity, which will mediate the relationship between the congruency of textures and purchase intent. We propose to investigate this assumption with the two studies presented below.

4.1.2 Online Sensory Information Processing: An Experimental Plan

Considering the upcoming *seamless* interactions consumers will experience in a near future with technologies (Pagani et al. 2019; Yadav and Pavlou 2014), the sensory similarity is important to consider for understanding how consumers process information with and through the interface consciously and unconsciously. Indeed, the closer an indirect or mediated experience is to the physical only experience of the product, the more the consumers' senses are stimulated and thus less likely in need to proceed high cognitive load to interpret, understand, evaluate and make a decision about the product. The full implication of the senses should lead to more natural and familiar interaction, enabling less learning stages and allow for a more flowing mediated interaction (Kock 2004, 2005).

4.1.2.1 Study 1—Evaluation of Realism Between Physical and Virtual Experiences of a Product

The first study we introduce below as a basis of our demonstration comes from Racat and Capelli (2016).[1] Along with the previous chapters, we develop our reasoning for a better understanding of consumer's perception and understanding of virtual products when interacting through

---

[1] For a complete version of the study, please refer to the article.

an interface. This first study presented allows to lie down the foundation for further investigating one of the specificity of the sense of touch which is the texture, the hardest characteristic to compute as previously explained. Therefore, this preliminary study aimed at investigating the effect of interacting with the product either physically or virtually—i.e. the consumer does not feel the product in hand neither its results but interacts with via a touchscreen interface—on consumers' satisfaction and perception of realism. Indeed, literature shows that innovative services and product adoption are likely to value consumers (Roehrich 2004) and that innovative behaviour is regarded according to a social system serving as a reference for comparing consumers' speed of adoption (Nyeck et al. 1996). Based on further literature in innovation and adoption behaviours, we suggested that (H1) consumers' satisfaction is superior when testing products with virtual try-on compared to the classical way. Besides, regarding consumers' concern with realism in virtual environment (Racat 2016), we also hypothesised that (H2a) the classical way to test a product presents higher degree of similarity than the virtual product testing, which (H2b) mediates the relation between the type of test and consumers' satisfaction such as the higher the degree of similarity, the higher the consumers' satisfaction. Finally, based on literature in marketing, we posited that (H3) the higher a consumer is satisfied of his or her product testing, the higher the intention to purchase is. We summarise our model with Fig. 4.1.

To test these hypotheses, we set up a between-subjects experiment with 111 valid participants after analysis who tested either physically or virtually a set of products. We chose the cosmetic sector as a product category due to the high tactile properties and the high rate of product

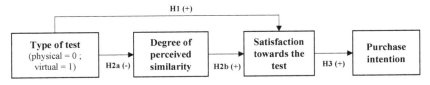

Fig. 4.1 Research model adapted from Racat and Capelli (2016)

sampling strategies. Accordingly, we configured a virtual make-up try-on that enables consumers to test different product on their face picture such as we obtain a basis of identical products to test between the virtual and physical conditions. Regarding the protocol, participants were randomly assigned to either the physical (N = 51) or the virtual product testing (N = 60) (i.e. participants used a former version of virtual make-up try-on such as Make-Up Genius[2]). Participants could take as long as wanted to use the proposed make-up (with sanitary conditions to remove and clean hands and faces). Finally, to measure the consumers' perception and responses, we used existing scale from the literature unless for the degree of similarity for which we developed a scale based on an exploratory study with 54 other consumers that routinely used cosmetics. In this exploratory phase (Racat 2016), consumers had the liberty to try-on products with a virtual make-up tool and then freely report their positive and negative experiences. From this material, we conducted a manual content analysis which allowed for determining verbatim corresponding to our conceptual definition of similarity.

Results indicate that, in the sequence type of test degree of similarity-satisfaction-purchase intention, the physical test induced higher perception of similarity compared to the virtual and thus leads to higher purchase intention. However, the direct effect of the virtual test leads to higher consumers' satisfaction regardless of the perceived similarity with the classical experience of product. Accordingly, results enabled us to corroborate H1 with the direct positive effect of the type of test and the satisfaction. Conversely, we observed a negative effect between these two same variables when the degree of similarity is introduced as a mediator such as the more physical is the test, the higher the degree of similarity while the similarity positively impacts consumers' satisfaction of the product test, as suggested by H2. Then results show an indirect mediation effect between the degree of similarity and the purchase intention through the satisfaction such as the direct effect between the degree of similarity and the purchase intention is not significant, which confirms H3. We summarise the results in Fig. 4.2.

---

[2]https://www.youtube.com/watch?v=zbBJfrkZRDI.

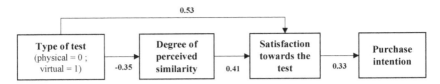

Fig. 4.2 Results of study 1

This first study enables to highlight the importance of the need for realism in consumers' online product testing. Indeed, findings confirm our predictions that the physical product testing is perceived as more realistic while the virtual product testing improves more consumers' satisfaction, which can be explained by utilitarian benefits (no contamination effect, possibility to test a large range of products, etc.) or hedonic benefits (effect of novelty with the virtual make-up try-on). According to this first result, we further investigate in a second study whether the direct tactile stimulation is used as a utilitarian experience (i.e. valued if similar to the direct sensory experience) or a hedonic experience (i.e. valued independently from the product presented on screen).

4.1.2.2 Study 2—Tactile Rendering to Serve Sensory Similarity of the Virtual Product Experience

This experiment is an original study where we explore the tactile dimension of the interface and the product and their effects on consumers' perception of realism. Precisely, we focus on the congruency of textures between the interface touch and the product tactile cues to variate sensory similarity and enhance consumers' perception of a realistic experience with the product.

Through the concept of sensory similarity that we described earlier, we propose to consider the processing of information, from a tactile perspective, thanks to the sensory cues induced such as direct tactile stimulation provided by an interface assists consumer decision-making by creating an online tactile experience of a product that resembles an offline experience with a product (i.e. hand manipulation). We propose that the online consumer product evaluation is related to the processing of sensory cues that will enhance sensory similarity, rather than a cognitive understanding of the product alone. Indeed, previous literature on the influence of tactile interfaces focuses only on the effect of tactile stimulation of the interface, not related to the product tactile cues (Shen et al. 2016). In this study, we focus on the effect of interface tactile stimulation related to the product texture on consumers' online product evaluation. We specifically search for understanding how the texture of an interface, which shares sensory cues with the product texture, influences consumers' response. Based on the above literature and our proposition, we suggest that the device used by the consumer to purchase a product should stimulate the sense of touch, to reproduce as closely as possible the physical experience of examining the product by hand. To enhance sensory similarity, there should be congruency between the tactile cues of the interface and the tactile cues of the product visualised on screen. When a consumer's online product manipulation experience is similar to a direct tactile product experience, the consumer is likely to value the examined product more highly (Daugherty et al. 2008). Indeed, research on online product manipulation shows that devices that offer vividness and interactivity enhance consumer experience and provide better product understanding (Jiang and Benbasat 2004); the more vivid and interactive the experience, the more the consumer perceives the online product manipulation to be analogue to a real product manipulation. Therefore, we contend that informational tactile stimulation—by which a device provides tactile cues about the product (i.e. congruency of texture)—increases sensory similarity, which mediates the relationship between the congruency of textures and attitude towards the product, such as (H1) the more the interface direct tactile stimulation is textured, the more it enhances consumer's attitude towards the product. Besides, (H2) congruency between interface tactile stimulation and product texture impacts the indirect effect of sensory similarity such that when the interface tactile stimulation and product texture match (mismatch), consumer response is enhanced (diminished). Also, texturing an interface should stimulate touch and provide useful, meaningful information regarding product characteristics for which consumers have a high instrumental need for touch (NFT) (McCabe and Nowlis 2003).

Fig. 4.3 Stimulus in 3D

Consequently, we hypothesise that (H3) the higher (lower) the consumer's instrumental NFT, the more positive the relationship between the congruency of textures and sensory similarity.

To test our hypothesis, we conducted a 2 (tablet screen—smooth and coarse) × 2 (product texture—cream and exfoliate) between-subjects experiment in a laboratory condition.

Materials and pretests. We used a dynamic 3D online product presentation to reproduce a spatial manipulation (Fig. 4.3). We selected products with high *touchability* (Brasel and Gips 2014). We chose two existing shower gel products (cream and exfoliate), for which we had a professional designer[3] to modify the texture of the original packaging to reproduce both the smooth and coarse sensations. We also modified the products' brand names to avoid brand bias effects and provided written descriptions of the products that were typical of descriptions of beauty

---

[3]Git Develipsum©, Patrice Ferlet.

products. We conducted a pretest to determine the visual-tactile perception of the two product stimuli. Ninety-four participants evaluated the products' textures (48 exfoliate and 46 cream) on a 7-point semantic differential scale with anchors of rough (1) to smooth (7) (Okamoto et al. 2013). The exfoliate shower gel was perceived significantly rougher than the cream shower gel ($M_{exfoliate} = 2.65$, $M_{cream} = 5.20$, $t = 8.061$, $p < 0.01$).

For the interfaces, we selected two digital tablets on which we applied modified screen protectors to manipulate the direct tactile stimulation (Fig. 4.4). We ran a pretest among 28 participants to evaluate the screen protector's textures on a 7-point semantic differential scale anchored by rough (1) to smooth (7). The smooth tactile stimulation was smoother than the coarse tactile stimulation ($M_{smooth\_stim} = 6.75$, $SD = 1.14$, $M_{coarse\_stim} = 1.86$, $SD = 1.15$, $t = 17.562$, $p < 0.001$). Participants concluded by matching product images and screen-textured samples; we obtained 89% of match between the smooth stimulation and the cream product ($M_{cream} = 1.11$ $SD = 0.32$, $t = 18.60$, $p < 0.001$) and 75% of match between the coarse stimulation and the exfoliate product ($M_{coarse} = 2.68$, $SD = 0.32$, $t = 20.61$, $p < 0.001$).

Participants and procedure. One hundred and forty-five female students from a Canadian university participated ($M_{age} = 23$, $SD = 5.45$) and were granted with a 5-Canadian dollar Amazon gift card. Participants were instructed to navigate to the webpage with the interface, where they were able to manipulate the product in 3D (360° rotation,

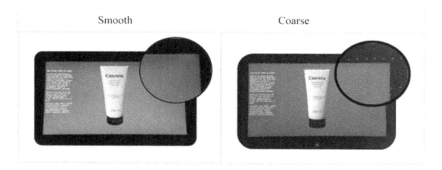

Fig. 4.4 Interface tactile stimuli—study 1

zooming in and out). A product description was also provided. Then participants filled out an online questionnaire.

Measures. The dependent variables were attitude towards the product, from Bergkvist and Rossiter (2007), and sensory similarity, for which we developed a scale focusing on sense of touch: (1) "*If I buy the product, I know I will have the same sensation*", (2) "*The product testing I realized is similar to a direct product testing*" and (3) "*I would have a better idea of product result if I could put some on my hands*". All measurements were made on a 7-point rating scale. We measured NFT with Peck and Childers (2003) scale. We controlled for product manipulation by adding written information on the back of the products, which we verified with a recognition method (Lwin et al. 2010). Finally, the first manipulation check was at the beginning of the questionnaire on products texture ("*The product seen on screen was... exfoliate* (1)-*cream* (7)") and the second at the end since it clearly referred to the texture of tablet screen ("*The screen of the tablet used was...Rough* (1)-*Smooth* (7)").

Results. First, with an exploratory factorial analysis, we validated the sensory similarity ($\alpha = 0.773$) and the attitude towards the product ($\alpha = 0.899$) measurement. Next, we ran the model 12 of the PROCESS macro from Hayes (2012) to test the direct effects on, and the mediating role of, sensory similarity between the interaction of textures and the attitude towards the product. Results showed a significant model ($F(7116) = 3.82$; $p = 0.009$). However, only the sensory similarity had a direct effect on attitude towards the product, which does not validate H1 on the direct effect of the interface texture on attitude towards the product. Moreover, instrumental NFT did not moderate the relation (p > 0.05) invalidating H3. Thus, we ran the analysis with the model 8 and controlled for the instrumental NFT. Results showed a significant model ($F(4119) = 6.37$; $p = 0.000$). The congruency of textures had a reversed effect on sensory similarity ($\beta_{congruency} = -0.81$, $t = -2.35$, $p = 0.020$). Besides, the interface tactile stimulation had a direct effect on sensory similarity ($\beta_{tactile\_stimulation} = 0.56$, $t = 2.25$, $p = 0.026$). Finally, we observed a direct effect of sensory similarity on attitude towards the product ($\beta_{similarity} = 0.37$, $t = 3.13$, $F(5118) = 3.98$, $p = 0.002$) and validated its mediating role ($\beta_{similarity} = -0.30$, CI [$-0.75$: -0.07]). Thus, due to the reversed direct effect of the congruency of textures on sensory similarity, we do not validate H2, but the latter mediated the relation: when the interface is smooth, the exfoliate product is better evaluated ($M_{\text{exfoliate}} = 4.92$; $M_{\text{cream}} = 4.15$; $t = -2.42$; $F(1, 60) = 1.53$; $p = 0.018$), while when the interface tactile stimulation is coarse, it is not significant. Plus, even if the direct effect of interface texture on attitude towards the product is not validated, we found a mediated effect via sensory similarity.

Discussion. This study validates the first test of the sensory similarity measure, from the tactile perspective, and assesses its mediation role in online browsing for products with high tactile cues. It shows that consumers consider both direct and indirect tactile stimulations when they interact with products through the interface and that such interaction positively influences their attitudes towards the products. However, the finding of a reversed effect with regard to textures shows that congruency between interface tactile stimulation and product cues does not result in higher perceived tactile similarity when textures match. In the online context, consumers are mainly stimulated with visual cues, which allow them to understand the product to proceed to purchase online (Hausman and Siekpe 2009). Yet we showed that when the interface directly stimulates the sense of touch, consumers better evaluate the product. Consequently, in online context, consumers consider the direct tactile stimulation, but they do not relate it to the product's tactile cues. The sensory similarity enhances consumers' online experiences and gives them more positive attitudes about products. However, familiarity of the consumers with one of the textures may have affected the results. The smooth tactile stimulation may be considered as a controlled condition rather than a real and full tactile stimulation as we introduced with the coarse condition.

4.2 Implication for the Future of Haptic Consumption

The two experiments presented in this chapter offer insightful perspectives for considering the question of realism into virtual consumption environments and particularly from the haptic lens. Findings of both studies suggest that consumers rely on tangible elements to procure reassurance on the potential or expected results of a product in physical interactions, while purchase intention is lower for virtual product testing. Specifically, in product testing situation, realism is important since the consumer relates to the outcomes that will indeed be once the product in hand for real use. Yet, when considering a more classical purchasing situation, consumers consider more the interface tactile cues rather than the direct relation between the touchscreen and the products. Thus, the interface tactile stimulation becomes a full part of the online consumers' experience as analogue to the physical experience of product where the product is the direct tactile stimulation. Yet these results need further investigation especially for the consideration of familiarity with the haptic rendering system.

Indeed, with the development of furthermore immersive devices and haptic possibilities, we need to question the fast-moving environment that push forward and force the consumer to rapidly adapt and evolve from the sensory perspective. Even though the lack of direct touch in mediated or virtual environments might seem non-natural for any type of interactions, as described throughout the previous chapters, direct tactile interactions can still be taken off an experience without disturbing fundamentally the consumers. Indeed, the latter will search and find alternative strategies for satisfying his or her needs for touch. Conversely, the more the haptic is considered in these environments, the less consumers are to perceive barriers to their tactile experiences since the interface becomes seamless and fully integrates the whole sensory processing of information. Furthermore, integrating haptic makes consumers to cognitively accept the mediation of interfaces that is necessary to reach out to products. This technical assumption is supported with upcoming technology as the example of the Go Touch VR Company which enables to realistically perceive textures in virtual environments (for further detail, see their website: https://www.gotouchvr.com/). Even more recently, the company HAP2U has been nominated as a Honouree for the CES 2020 edition for their haptic rendering technology integrated into "as-we-know" touch-based devices as tablet or smartphones (for further detail, see their website: https://www.hap2u.net/). In particular, they enable touchscreens to actually render textures as if it was a direct and physical interaction.

Therefore, despite the relative low familiarity with haptic technologies, consumers are familiar enough with technologies that require both their touch and voice to command, control and further interact virtually with people and objects. Nevertheless, new introduction to the market as Alexa or Google Home shakes the potential future of haptic technologies and their real interest/use in future mediated environments. In the 2000s, the introduction of tactile devices provided hope for larger place to use tactile interactions but, unfortunately, the devices were limited to rather soft rendering and simple type of interfaces (Parisi 2018a). Once more, following immersive environments, which further emphasise the need for stimulating the whole sensory system especially the sense of touch, we posit the question of what is the main consideration for human understanding of his environment? It has been long demonstrated that a world without the sense of touch is not possible for many reasons related mostly to social needs and existence definition. However, introducing haptic rendering also means new consideration of touch as well as new definition of touching (Parisi 2014; Debrégeas et al. 2009; Parisi 2018b). As an evolving species, the nature of touch and its functions have been drastically modified in about 30 years. Designing interfaces supposed choosing ways for interacting in the future. Thus, what will it be? Will touch be part of it? Or should we choose to believe that we can despise it and overcome its influence?

Along with the development of the book, we have based all our thinking on a prospective approach to the implementation of a new technology: tactile rendering, considering that the role of the researcher is to anticipate changes in purchasing and consumption patterns. However, if we take this prospective logic further, the use of the theory of embodiment is questionable in the context of online purchasing. Indeed, if current generations refer to a physical experience for real purchase that has generated and defined their buying experience, one can imagine that this real experience will not necessarily be the norm for the next generation of buyers as online and physical environments have been existing since they were born (after 1995/2000: generation Z, digital natives, etc.). Will future generations still have an "embodied" shopping experience? If so, the question of sensory similarity will no longer be relevant since these individuals will only seek similarity with their other past online shopping experiences. However, products will also evolve as we probably no longer use all tangible objects as we currently do, in particular, if we consider reducing pollution. Yet the difference will probably still exist between physical and tangible products and virtuals. Therefore, the question that may rise would be to define a virtual product and its sensory cues? In this case, it is the consumption or use situation of the product that could then serve as a reference to establish a sensory similarity between two experiences. This question requires future research to establish a link, no longer between actual purchase and online purchase, but between consumption and online purchase.

Still from a prospective perspective, we nowadays call "interfaces" the tools that allow us to interact in a virtual environment: they are intermediaries with whom we are in conscious sensory contact. However, in the future, technologies could be fully integrated into humans and thus no longer go through sensory contact by directly stimulating the brain (without the help of sensory sensors). In this future, there would no longer be an interface as such, which would deprive the customer of direct contact during the purchase, and make consumption the only moment of sensory stimulation related to the product. In particular, current virtual head-mounted system tends to "fool" the brain to recreate a certain reality. Accordingly, would our senses still be reliable and useful? The sense of touch remains the only connecting sense. Should we give the right attention to it before getting off reality?

References

Aaker, David, and Kevin Keller. 1990. "Consumer Evaluations of Brand Extensions." *Journal of Marketing* 54 (1): 27–41.
Barsalou, Lawrence W. 1999. "Perceptual Symbol System." *Behavioral and Brain Sciences* 22: 577–660. https://doi.org/10.1098/rstb.2003.1319.
———. 2008. "Grounded Cognition." *Annual Review of Psychology* 59 (1): 617–45. https://doi.org/10.1146/annurev.psych.59.103006.093639.

———. 2010. "Grounded Cognition: Past, Present, and Future." *Topics in Cognitive Science* 2 (4): 716–24. https://doi.org/10.1111/j.1756-8765.2010.01115.x.
Bergkvist, L., and J. R. Rossiter. 2007. "The Predictive Validity of Multiple-Item Versus Single-Item Measures of the Same Constructs." *Journal of Marketing Research* 44 (2): 175–84.
Bèzes, C., and M. Mercanti-Guérin. 2016. "La similarité en marketing: périmètre, mesure et champs d'application." *Recherche et Applications en Marketing* (French ed.) 32 (1): 86–109.
Brasel, S. Adam, and James Gips. 2014. "Tablets, Touchscreens, and Touchpads: How Varying Touch Interfaces Trigger Psychological Ownership and Endowment." *Journal of Consumer Psychology* 24 (2): 226–33. https://doi.org/10.1016/j.jcps.2013.10.003.
———. 2015. "Interface Psychology: Touchscreens Change Attribute Importance, Decision Criteria, and Behavior in Online Choice." *Cyberpsychology, Behavior, and Social Networking* 18 (9): 534–38. https://doi.org/10.1089/cyber.2014.0546.
Daugherty, Terry, Hairong Li, and Frank Biocca. 2008. "Consumer Learning and the Effects of Virtual Experience Relative to Indirect and Direct Product Experience." *Psychology & Marketing* 25 (7): 568–86. https://doi.org/10.1002/mar.20225.
Debrégeas, Georges, Alexis Prevost, and Julien Scheibert. 2009. "Toucher Digital Humain : Transduction Mécanique de l'information Tactile et Rôle Des Empreintes Digitales." *Images de La Physique*, 11–17.
Dimofte, Claudiu V., Mark R. Forehand, and Rohit Deshpandé. 2003. "Ad Schema Incongruity As Elicitor of Ethnic Self-Awareness and Differential Advertising Response." *Journal of Advertising* 32 (4): 7–17. https://doi.org/10.1080/00913367.2003.10639142.
Fleck, Nathalie, and Virginie Maille. 2010. "Trente Ans de Travaux Contradictoires Sur l'influence de La Congruence Perçue Par Le Consommateur: Synthèse, Limites et Voies de Recherche." *Recherche et Applications En Marketing* 25 (4): 69–92.
Gentner, D., and V. Gunn. 2001. "Structural Alignment Facilitates the Noticing of Differences." *Memory & Cognition* 29 (4): 565–77.
Goodman, G. S. 1980. "Picture Memory: How the Action Schema Affects Retention." *Cognitive Psychology* 12 (4): 473–95. https://doi.org/10.1016/0010-0285(80)90017-1.
Grohmann, Bianca, Eric R. Spangenberg, and David E. Sprott. 2007. "The Influence of Tactile Input on the Evaluation of Retail Product Offerings."

Journal of Retailing 83 (2): 237–45. https://doi.org/10.1016/j.jretai.2006.09.001.

Grundwald, Martin. 2008. *Human Haptic Perception: Basic and Applications*. Edited by Martin Grundwald. Berlin: Birkhäuser.

Gueorguiev, David, Eric Vezzoli, André Mouraux, Betty Lemaire-Semail, and Jean Louis Thonnard. 2017. "The Tactile Perception of Transient Changes in Friction." *Journal of the Royal Society Interface* 14 (137). https://doi.org/10.1098/rsif.2017.0641.

Hausman, Angela V., and Jeffrey Sam Siekpe. 2009. "The Effect of Web Interface Features on Consumer Online Purchase Intentions." *Journal of Business Research* 62 (1): 5–13.

Hayes, A. F. 2012. PROCESS: A Versatile Computational Tool for Observed Variable Mediation, Moderation, and Conditional Process Modeling (White Paper).

Heckler, Susan E., and Terry L. Childers. 1992. "The Role of Expectancy and Relevancy in Memory for Verbal and Visual Information: What Is Incongruency?" *Journal of Consumer Research* 18 (4): 475. https://doi.org/10.1086/209275.

Heit, E. 1997. "Features of Similarity and Category-Based Induction." An Interdisciplinary Workshop on Similarity and Categorisation (SimCat).

Jiang, Zhenhui, and Izak Benbasat. 2004. "Virtual Product Experience: Effects of Visual and Functional Control of Products on Perceived Diagnosticity and Flow in Electronic Shopping." *Journal of Management Information Systems* 21 (3): 111–47. https://doi.org/10.1080/07421222.2004.11045817.

Kock, Ned. 2004. "The Psychobiological Model: Towards a New Theory of Computer-Mediated Communication Based on Darwinian Evolution." *Organization Science* 15 (3): 327–48. https://doi.org/10.1287/orsc.1040.0071.

———. 2005. "Media Richness or Media Naturalness? The Evolution of Our Biological Communication Apparatus and Its Influence on Our Behavior toward e-Communication Tools." *IEEE Transactions on Professional Communication* 48 (2): 117–30. https://doi.org/10.1109/TPC.2005.849649.

Lwin, May O., Maureen Morrin, and Aradhna Krishna. 2010. "Exploring the Superadditive Effects of Scent and Pictures on Verbal Recall: An Extension of Dual Coding Theory." *Journal of Consumer Psychology* 20 (3): 317–26.

Maille, Virginie, and Nathalie Fleck. 2011. "Congruence Perçue Par Le Consommateur: Vers Une Clarification Du Concept, de Sa Formation et de Sa Mesure." *Recherche et Applications En Marketing* 26 (2): 77–111.

McCabe, Deborah Brown, and Stephen M. Nowlis. 2003. "The Effect of Examining Actual Products or Product Descriptions on Consumer Preference." *Journal of Consumer Psychology* 13 (4): 431–39. https://doi.org/10.1207/S15327663JCP1304_10.

Meyers-Levy, Joan, and Alice M. Tybout. 1989. "Schema Congruity as a Basis for Product Evaluation." *Journal of Consumer Research* 16 (1): 39–54. https://doi.org/10.1086/647521.

Montagu, Ashley. 1971. *Touching: The Human Significance of the Skin*. New York, NY: Columbia University.

Nyeck, Simon, Sylvie Paradis, Jean-Marc Xuereb, and Jean-Charles Chebat. 1996. "Standardisation Ou Adaptation Des Échelles de Mesure à Travers Différents Contextes Nationaux: L'exemple d'une Échelle de Mesure de l'innovativité." *Recherche et Applications En Marketing* 11 (3): 57–74. http://ram.sagepub.com/content/11/3/57.short.

Okamoto, Shogo, Hikaru Nagano, and Yoji Yamada. 2013. "Psychophysical Dimensions of Tactile Perception of Textures." *IEEE Transactions on Haptics* 6 (1): 81–93.

Pagani, Margherita, Margot Racat, and Charles F. Hofacker. 2019. "Adding Voice to the Omnichannel and How That Affects Brand Trust." *Journal of Interactive Marketing* 48: 89–105. https://doi.org/10.1016/j.intmar.2019.05.002.

Parisi, David. 2014. "Reach In and Feel Something: On the Strategic Reconstruction of Touch in Virtual Space." *Animation: An Interdisciplinary Journal* 9 (2): 228–44. https://doi.org/10.1177/1746847714527195.

———. 2018a. *Archaeologies of Touch: Interfacing with Haptics from Electricity to Computing*. University of Minnesota Press.

———. 2018b. "Tactile Modernity: On the Rationalization of Touch in the Nineteenth Century." January.

Parisi, David, and Jason E. Archer. 2017. "Making Touch Analog : The Prospects and Perils of a Haptic Media Studies." https://doi.org/10.1177/1461444817717517.

Park, C. Whan, Sandra Milberg, and Robert Lawson. 1991. "Evaluation of Brand Extensions: The Role of Product Feature Similarity and Brand Concept Consistency." *Journal of Consumer Research* 18 (2): 185–93. https://doi.org/10.2307/2489554.

Peck, Joann, and Terry L. Childers. 2003. "Individual Differences in Haptic Information Processing: The 'Need for Touch' Scale." *Journal of Consumer Research* 30 (3): 430–43.

Racat, Margot. 2016. "L'influence de La Stimulation Tactile Lors de l'évaluation En Ligne d'un Produit." University of Lyon.

Racat, Margot, and Sonia Capelli. 2016. "L'impact de La Similarité Sur l'efficacité Des Outils d'aide à La Vente En Ligne." *Revue Francaise de Gestion* 254 (1): 89–105. https://doi.org/10.3166/rfg.2016.00005.

Roehrich, Gilles. 2004. "Consumer Innovativeness Concepts and Measurements." *Journal of Business Research* 57 (6): 671–77. https://doi.org/10.1016/S0148-2963(02)00311-9.

Rosa, José Antonio, and Alan J. Malter. 2003. "E-(Embodied) Knowledge and E-Commerce: How Physiological Factors Affect Online Sales of Experiential Products." *Journal of Consumer Psychology* 13 (1–2): 63–73.

Sagi, E., D. Gentner, and A. Lovett. 2012. "What Difference Reveals about Similarity." *Cognitive Science* 36 (6): 1019–50.

Shen, Hao, Meng Zhang, and Aradhna Krishna. 2016. "Computer Interfaces and the 'Direct-Touch' Effect: Can IPads Increase the Choice of Hedonic Food?" *Journal of Marketing Research* 53 (5): 745–58.

Shepard, Roger N. 1964. "Attention and the Metric Structure of the Stimulus Space." *Journal of Mathematical Psychology* 1 (1): 54–87. https://doi.org/10.1016/0022-2496(64)90017-3.

Taylor, E. G., and J. E. Hummel. 2007. "Perspectives on Similarity from the LISA Model." *Analogies: Integrating Multiple Cognitive Abilities* 5: 21.

Torgerson, W. S. 1965. "Multidimensional Scaling of Similarity." *Psychometrika* 30 (4): 379–93.

Tversky, A., and I. Gati. 1978. "Studies of Similarity." *Cognition and Categorization* 1 (1978): 79–98.

Unger, Bertram, Ralph Hollis, and Roberta Klatzky. 2011. "Roughness Perception in Virtual Textures." *IEEE Transactions on Haptics* 4 (2): 122–33. https://doi.org/10.1109/TOH.2010.61.

Yadav, Manjit S., and Paul A. Pavlou. 2014. "Marketing in Computer-Mediated Environments: Research Synthesis and New Directions." *Journal of Marketing* 78 (1): 20–40. https://doi.org/10.1509/jm.12.0020.

Zhu, Ying, and Jeffrey Meyer. 2017. "Getting in Touch with Your Thinking Style: How Touchscreens Influence Purchase." *Journal of Retailing and Consumer Services* 38 (September): 51–58. https://doi.org/10.1016/j.jretconser.2017.05.006.

Conclusion

After almost three decades now, marketers have reached a critical understanding of the importance of consumers' senses into the processing of brands, products and advertising information. So far, most of research and books published on the topics highlight how the use of senses can trigger sales of a product in physical environments. However, the development of Internet since the 1990s early questioned the possibilities for marketers and consumers to reach out the product in different environments. First considered as two different environments, the physical and virtual shopping channels, enabled via technological settings, rapidly became complementary or even merged to provide a full consumer's product or brand experience. Furthermore, research in sensory marketing rubs it in since, at first glance, only two senses can directly be stimulated—the visual and sound senses—from an occidental perspective of the senses. Yet, recent advances in technologies tend to enable sensations able to render or stimulate physical sensations that would be similar to the handling of the same product. These emerging possibilities question the way consumers are and will be able to feel a product according to the reality it relies on. As well, it also gives a new position of reference to dig deeper into the consumer psychology from an

© The Editor(s) (if applicable) and The Author(s), under exclusive license to Springer Nature Switzerland AG 2020
M. Racat and S. Capelli, *Haptic Sensation and Consumer Behaviour*,
https://doi.org/10.1007/978-3-030-36922-4

information processing perspective: How does the sensory information influence the consumer's behaviour when it apparently cannot reach out the product? The present book offered a frame of reference of the most relevant research linking the senses to both environments—physical and virtual—and how it is processed by consumers to evaluate, judge and act. Particularly, a special focus on the haptic sensations has been given since this area of research benefits from a large attention by engineering and technical sciences while, from the marketing perspective, it remains an accessory sense into consumers' experience despite numerous examples of its use and benefits in the marketing literature.

Index

A

Ability 12, 37, 42, 69, 78, 80, 99
Abstract 69
Academics ix, 1, 4, 7, 9, 43, 51, 66
Acquisition 100
Actual 50, 51, 69, 70, 79–81, 112
Addiction 70
Age 2, 6
Algorithm 80
Anisotropy 80
Anxiety 5
Apprehension x, 2, 11, 17, 19, 22, 36, 51, 66, 68, 70, 74, 81
Approach ix, xi, 5, 11, 34, 37, 39, 42, 43, 47, 73, 79–83, 95, 111
Appropriateness 98
Attitude 3, 19, 78, 105, 108, 109
Augmented reality xi, 34, 40
Augmented virtuality 40
Autotelic 12, 82

B

Barrier 4, 22, 36, 37, 70, 110
Behaviour ix, x, 3–6, 9–11, 13–15, 18–22, 36, 41, 50, 69, 70, 75, 79, 80, 82, 102
Bilateral signal communication 72, 73
Biological 70
Brands 11, 13, 15, 19, 20, 35, 47, 68, 73, 106

C

Channel 35
Characteristics x, 1, 2, 9–11, 13–16, 18, 37, 40, 43, 50, 73, 102, 105
Choice 13, 20, 66
Cognitive x, 16, 51, 98–101, 105
Common 5, 17, 98, 99

Index

Communication 6, 42, 45, 68
Comprehension 4, 74
Computer x, 18, 34, 39, 43, 47, 50, 51, 67, 70, 75, 96
Computer-mediated 38, 42, 69, 79
Computer sciences 40, 42, 43, 72, 75
Confidence 18, 20, 50, 66
Congruence/congruency/congruent 96–100, 105, 109
Connect 2, 4, 6, 7, 9, 35, 49, 73
Consumer/consumers xi, 10, 11, 13–15, 17, 18, 20–22, 33–43, 47–51, 66–70, 73, 75, 78–82, 84, 96–98, 100–105, 109–111
Consumption xi, 1, 6, 10, 12, 14, 16, 21, 22, 34, 39, 47, 67, 70–72, 81, 82, 84, 95, 97, 112
Contagion 21, 22
Contamination 20–22, 49, 104
Contouring 74, 80
Control 37, 43, 44, 67, 70, 80, 111
Cultural 1, 5, 12, 13, 22, 72
Cutaneous 8, 9, 44, 75, 81

D

Dematerialization 16, 35, 39
Diagnostic 17, 18, 37, 40, 84
Difference 5, 19, 69, 97, 99, 100, 112
Digital xi, 16, 34, 35, 40, 72, 96, 107, 111
Dimension 2, 5, 8, 12, 14, 17, 19, 20, 22, 41–43, 51, 69, 74, 79, 83, 84, 104
Direct 2, 7, 35, 39, 47, 48, 52, 67, 69, 75, 79, 80, 82, 97, 100, 103–105, 107–112

Dissociation 4, 8, 70, 97
Distinctive 81
Dynamic 10, 37, 38, 49

E

Electricity 71
Embodied cognition 99
Engagement 68
Environment/environments ix, x, 2, 3, 6, 7, 9–11, 14–16, 19, 22, 33–43, 45, 47–52, 66, 69–71, 78, 79, 81–84, 97–100, 109–111
Evaluation 4, 11, 13, 17–21, 48, 50, 52, 77, 100, 105
Evolution x, 7, 33, 34, 39, 48, 49, 84
Existence 3, 38, 111
Experience/experiential ix, xi, 2, 11, 15, 19, 34–40, 42, 43, 45–49, 52, 66, 67, 70–73, 75, 78, 79, 82–84, 96–98, 100, 101, 103–105, 110, 112
Experiment 3, 20, 69, 71, 83, 84, 102, 104, 106, 109
Exploratory procedures 17, 18
Extension 79, 96

F

Familiarity 68, 109–111
Features 47, 49, 73
Feelings 3, 14, 20–22, 43, 52, 67, 79, 82
Female 4, 107
Fingers 44, 52, 74, 76, 77, 80
Fit 22, 98
Force 10, 71, 72, 74, 110

Force feedback 72, 74, 75, 80
Formats 37, 48, 49
Friction 19, 72, 74, 81
Frustration 38
Functioning 18, 71
Future xi, 14, 75, 81, 84, 95, 101, 111, 112

G

Gender 4, 5, 13, 22
Geometric/geometrical 15–18, 37, 38, 51, 66, 73, 74, 81, 84
Gestures 69, 82
Grounded cognition 99
Grounded cognition theory 69, 97

H

Hand manipulation 104
Hand/hands 3–5, 7–9, 11, 17, 22, 37, 52, 68, 69, 72, 75, 97, 98, 100, 102, 103, 105, 110
Haptic 8–10, 17–19, 22, 34, 37, 38, 42, 43, 47, 50, 51, 67, 69, 71, 72, 74, 77, 81, 84, 109, 110
Haptic consumption 109
Haptic information 12, 66
Harlow, Harry 2
Hedonic 12, 16, 67, 68, 97
Hold 37, 68
Human–machine 38, 39, 42
Hypothesis 98, 102, 106

I

Image/images 21, 35–38, 48–51, 67, 78, 82
Image interactivity 36, 42, 48, 49, 67, 80–82, 84

Imaginary 22, 37, 41, 82, 83, 96, 111
Immersion 41–43, 47, 82
Immersive 37, 43, 45, 83, 110
Implication 22, 41, 101
Improvement 71, 73
Inability 34, 38, 49
Indirect 39, 47, 69, 97, 100, 101, 103, 105, 109
Individual 4, 5, 8, 10–15, 20, 78, 82, 83, 99, 112
Influence x, 2, 3, 6, 9, 11, 14, 18–22, 41, 43, 66–68, 70, 72, 74, 75, 79, 84, 100, 105, 109, 111
Information x, 7–12, 15–18, 35, 36, 50, 68, 73, 74, 97, 99, 100, 105, 108
Initiate 4, 5, 17
In-store 11–13, 20, 21, 34, 48–50, 79, 97, 100
Instrumental 12
Intangibility 36, 37
Integration 39–41
Interacting/interaction/interactions ix, x, 4, 6, 7, 9, 13–15, 20, 22, 33–43, 47–50, 67–70, 72, 73, 75, 79–81, 96, 97, 99–102, 108–111
Interactivity 36, 37, 47, 48, 80, 82, 105
Interface x, xi, 6, 14, 22, 34, 36–43, 47, 50, 65–72, 74, 75, 79, 82, 84, 96, 97, 100–102, 104, 105, 107–112
Interfaces touch 82, 96, 104
Intermediaries x, 65, 112
Internet x, 13, 14, 33–36, 38–40, 43, 48, 50, 66

Internet of Things ix, 49, 70
Interpersonal 4, 5
Interplay 51
Intimate 4
Investigation 14, 22, 110
Involvement 67

Judgement 18, 20, 50, 66, 79

Knowledge 4, 8, 14, 21, 35, 71, 78, 98–100

Limbs 8, 10, 71
Literal similarity 98
Load 37, 39, 51, 70, 101

Male 4, 5
Manipulation 36, 43, 44, 66, 69, 74, 80, 97, 100, 101, 105, 106, 108
Marketers ix, x, 15, 34, 47–50, 66
Match-up 98
Material xi, 6, 15–20, 38, 51, 71, 81, 84, 95, 96, 103
Mechanical 9, 10, 37, 72, 75, 83
Mechanical signals 71
Mechanism 8, 9, 43, 71, 96, 97
Mediated/mediation x, 22, 39, 42, 43, 47, 66, 68, 69, 101, 103, 109, 110
Mental 7, 17, 37, 69, 97, 99

Merging ix, x, 14, 39, 70, 78
Midas touch 4, 69
Mimic 96, 100
Mouse 14, 43, 44, 52, 66, 67, 77
Movements 10, 17, 37, 44, 71, 72, 77, 81, 83
Multichannel 47
Multisensory 68, 81, 83

Natural 6, 37–39, 42, 68, 70, 73, 84, 101
Navigation 37, 43, 44, 82
Need for tactile information 3, 4, 6, 18
Need for touch (NFT) 11–14, 20, 37, 38, 52, 73, 105, 106, 108
Nervous system 7, 9
Neuronal 99

Offline 15, 49, 104
Online 6, 13, 15, 35–37, 42, 48–51, 67, 70, 80, 82, 96, 97, 100, 101, 104, 105, 108–112
Online interaction 67
Organs 7–9, 69, 100
Ownership 20, 52, 67, 82

Pad 43, 67
Paradox 33
People 4–7, 22, 35, 40, 41, 43, 69, 70, 97, 111
Perceived similarity 103, 109
Perception/perceptual ix, x, 2–4, 6–10, 14, 19, 21, 22, 39, 42,

43, 48, 50, 66, 68, 72, 73, 76, 77, 79, 84, 96, 97, 99–104, 107
Physical x, 3, 15, 22, 35, 36, 39, 43, 49, 66, 69–71, 80, 101, 103, 112
Physical reality x, 35, 36, 40, 42, 69, 72, 79
Physiological 7, 96
Presence 43, 45, 46, 82
Presentation 11, 37, 48, 49, 106
Process 2, 9, 20, 49, 68, 71, 99–101, 108
Processing 14, 72, 74, 78, 97, 100
Processing of information 7, 65, 104, 110
Product ix, x, 2, 8–22, 33–40, 42, 43, 47–52, 65–70, 73–75, 78–80, 84, 96–110, 112
Product image 51, 67, 107
Product testing 48, 49, 102–104, 110
Product touch 13–15, 19, 20, 34, 38, 40, 47, 51, 66
Properties 15, 17–21, 38, 51, 81, 102
Prospective 111
Psychological 1, 3, 22, 42, 43, 47, 82, 84, 97
Psychological transfer 69
Psychophysical 2, 19, 74
Purchase 12, 13, 19–21, 34–36, 39, 48–50, 66, 67, 79, 96, 100–103, 105, 109–112

R

Rational 67, 97

Real 16, 22, 35, 45, 47, 49, 52, 68, 70, 76, 96, 97, 100, 101, 105, 109–111
Real-based 96
Realism/realistic 48, 78–81, 84, 97, 102, 104, 109, 110
Realistic sensations 73
Realities/reality 6, 22, 38, 40–42, 78, 80, 82, 83, 112
Reception 7, 10, 73
Receptor 7–10
Recovering 66, 71
Relatedness 98
Relational 3, 4, 39, 98
Relational similarity 98
Relationship 4, 7, 38, 39, 42, 96, 101, 105, 106
Rendering 47, 72–75, 78–82, 110, 111
Representation 6, 8, 15, 17, 37, 47, 67, 69, 72, 77, 80, 99
Reproduce 79, 100, 105, 106
Retrieve 37, 38, 79
Revolution x, 38
Rich 36

S

Satisfaction 49, 102–104
Screen 51, 52, 66, 67, 83, 96, 98, 100, 104, 105, 107
Seamless 39, 67, 73, 101, 110
Seamlessly 49, 70, 71
Sensation/sensations 7, 8, 21, 37, 38, 43, 72, 75, 79–81, 84, 100, 106
Sense/senses/sensory ix, x, 2–4, 6, 8, 9, 15–18, 21, 22, 36–40, 42, 47–50, 66, 68, 69, 71, 72,

78–84, 96, 97, 99–101, 105, 110, 112
Sensitivity 7, 9, 10, 66
Sensory information processing 97, 98, 101
Sensory modalities 68, 81
Sensory stimulation 35, 37, 39–42, 82, 96, 112
Sensory system 17, 111
Shopping xi, 11–13, 18, 21, 34, 51, 52, 65
Similarity 97–106, 108, 109, 112
Skin 3, 8–10, 75
Smartphone 34, 39, 43, 44, 48, 50, 68, 70, 73, 110
Social 4, 6, 12, 13, 15, 22, 70, 102, 111
Static 10, 36–38
Stimulate/stimuli/stimulation ix, 7, 10, 14, 36, 38, 42, 43, 47, 48, 50–52, 67, 68, 71, 75, 76, 79, 81, 83, 84, 96, 107
Stress 3, 5
Stroking gestures 82
Suitability 98
Swipe 70

T

Tablet x, 34, 39, 43, 44, 50, 52, 67, 70, 72, 73, 107, 110
Tactile xi, 2, 4–6, 9, 11, 14, 19, 39, 43, 48–50, 52, 66–73, 75, 79, 80, 84, 96, 100, 104
Tactile attributes 19, 65
Tactile rendering xi, 65, 71, 72, 79, 81, 84, 96, 111
Tactile sensation 2, 4, 7, 8, 14, 18, 51, 52, 70, 79, 80, 96

Tactile stimulation 8, 13, 18–20, 50–52, 73, 75, 81, 82, 101, 104, 105, 107–110
Talking 5, 43, 68
Tangible x, 6, 40, 51, 52, 66, 78–80, 99, 110, 112
Tape 70
Techniques xi, 19, 65, 71, 72, 74, 75
Technologies/technology ix, x, 6, 7, 22, 33–39, 41, 45, 47–51, 70–72, 78–84, 100, 101, 110–112
Texture 9, 15, 16, 19, 20, 50–52, 73–76, 79–81, 96, 100–102, 104–111
Thinking style 67
Torques 71
Touch x, 1–9, 11–14, 16–18, 21, 22, 34, 40, 49–51, 66–68, 71, 75, 76, 79, 97, 99, 100, 102, 105, 108–112
Touch-ability 51, 52, 106
Touchscreens 14, 43, 67, 68, 70, 72, 79, 80, 82, 102, 110, 111
Transmission 7
Trust 4, 12, 66, 68, 70

U

Utilitarian 12, 16, 67, 68, 97, 104

V

Virtual ix–xi, 75, 81, 83, 103, 112
Virtually 48, 68, 102, 111
Virtual consumption 34, 41, 66, 79–81, 109
Virtual environments ix–xi, 11, 13, 14, 22, 34, 39–41, 43, 47,

67–69, 71, 73, 75, 78–80, 84, 97, 102, 110, 112
Virtual objects 69, 72, 73
Virtual product experience 37
Virtual reality (VR) x, 35, 40, 41, 43, 45, 72, 79, 96, 97
Virtual representation 80
Virtual test 103
Virtual try-on 37, 48, 49, 96, 102

Visual 2, 3, 9, 17, 42, 44, 47, 51, 67, 79, 81, 96
Visualisation 37, 40
Visual-tactile 51, 107
Vivid/vividness 36, 37, 42, 70, 101, 105
Vocal commands 39, 68

Z

Zone 4

CPSIA information can be obtained
at www.ICGtesting.com
Printed in the USA
LVHW032342110121
676226LV00004B/248